# CRYSTAL HEALING
 *a beginner's guide*

ROGER CROXSON

D1514110

*Headway* · Hodder & Stoughton

Order queries: please contact Bookpoint Ltd, 39 Milton Park,
Abingdon, Oxon OX14 4TD. Telephone: (44) 01235 400414,
Fax: (44) 01235 400454. Lines are open from 9.00 - 6.00, Monday to
Saturday, with a 24 hour message answering service.
Email address: orders@bookpoint.co.uk

*British Library Cataloguing in Publication Data*
A catalogue record for this title is available from The British Library

ISBN 0 340 73065 X

First published 1999
Impression number   10  9  8  7  6  5  4  3  2  1
Year                      2004  2003  2002  2001  2000  1999

Copyright © 1999 Roger Croxson

Typeset by Transet Limited, Coventry, England.
Printed in Great Britain for Hodder & Stoughton Educational, a division
of Hodder Headline plc, 338 Euston Road, London NW1 3BH by
Cox & Wyman Limited, Reading, Berkshire.

# CONTENTS

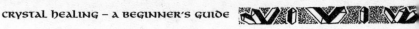

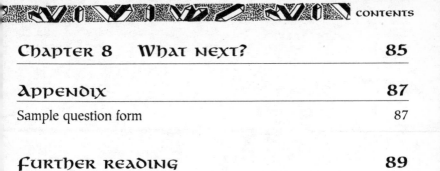

# INTRODUCTION TO CRYSTAL HEALING

*Welcome to this beginner's guide to crystal healing; its objective is to enable you simply to use basic crystal healing at home on friends and family in a safe and enjoyable way. It may also help you to increase your intuitive and other abilities. It has been written for those who do not have any crystals as well as those who have a collection on the mantleshelf. The idea of this book is to encourage you to teach yourself, become familiar with the techniques and for you to go forward to more practical training. This is achieved by providing techniques that you apply to the situation in which you find yourself; this puts you in control of what you do. Any of the techniques described in this book are for family and friends, with their consent and understanding that you are not trained in healing. You should also state that you do not have any liability insurance (held by professional crystal healers). You should also suggest that they seek professional medical assistance for any medical problems. This form of complementary therapy must not be used as a substitute for professional medical treatment.*

Most chapters describe one or more particular processes and, at the end of each chapter, there is a space to practise these exercises. Some of these are presented in the form of a summary of the chapter, giving the essential guidelines. Where possible, apart from the crystals, everyday items are used, hopefully things that are easily available. Although it is not always possible, the use of specialized words has been kept to a minimum and, where necessary, key words have been described. There is no uniform to wear and no special place to work. There is information on how to turn your living room into a healing room and just as importantly

1

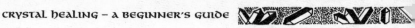

how to reverse the process. This is 'everyday kitchen table' crystal healing, so that you can work with crystals when and where needed.

There are no rules unless necessary for safety and reasons of health; using vibrational medicine in healing is very much a personal interpretation. There are certain safeguards for both you and the person on whom you are working. Beyond these, the way you work and interpret the crystals is the way you are. We all talk, walk and function in different ways; so we can all help in different ways and use crystals in different ways. There may be as many different ways of providing crystal healing as there are crystal healers. Therefore, what you read is designed to be a guide which you then use to your best advantage. These ideas are not set in stone.

This book neither gives lists of properties of crystals and gemstones nor what they will cure or treat. This is for three reasons. First, one of the main objectives is to get used to crystals and how to look after them and the best way is by practical experience. Second, some of the healing will be with clear quartz and specific sets of crystals. Third, the idea is to teach you how to find out the properties of crystals with out looking them up in a book, unless it is to check your own findings. This is because each stone is slightly different as is each situation where you will want to use them. Also each person, and how they use crystals, is different. Once you understand a crystal then look it up but apply what other people say to your own base knowledge.

At this stage you will not work at a great depth or on anyone with a serious illness; if you or the person you are working with has a medical condition, physical or emotional, then consult a qualified medical practitioner. You need to be able to select and use an effective crystal healing process, that relates to the situation and it will be only you who can assess what is needed at that time, not a book. Therefore, the use of your own judgement and belief in your intuition is important.

Note the terms *crystal*, *stone* and *gemstone* are all used interchangeably, this is to decrease the repetition of various words.

# LISTEN TO YOURSELF

We all have intuitive abilities; although often maligned they are part of our life. Everyday speech with such statements as 'women's intuition' or 'I knew it was going to be you' shows that these processes are part of our society's make up. This potential to sense certain things is often considered more of a female skill than male. In reality, there is no reason why men cannot be as intuitive as women are, there may be physical differences, but a lot of the difference is from the way children are brought up. These are general statements but when you look around at the way most children are treated, then the difference becomes apparent. Our intuition is the ability to know who is on the other end of the telephone before picking up the handset, or that a partner has

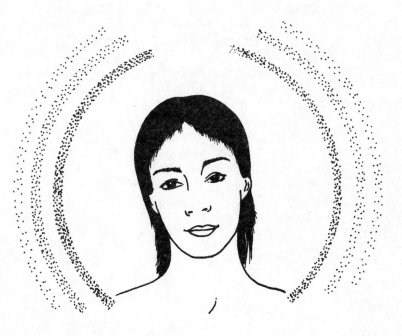

**Figure 1** Everyone is a healer

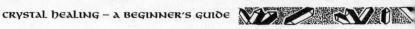

missed the train and not to put the meal on for another 30 minutes. We can, with care, utilize these abilities within our crystal work, whether we choose to train ourselves to increase our potential is a major question that only we can answer. We have to learn to listen to that little voice inside that is so often correct. If you think it is imagination, remember how many times it has been right before the event; trust yourself! Also the definition of imagination is only one developed by that part of society that likes every thing to have good scientific backing. Can we really separate intuition from imagination?

So now is the time to decide whether or not you will start to listen to your intuition and believe in your abilities. This does not mean that you do everything that the little voice in your head says. Remember we are still bound by both moral and legal codes.

One result of listening to yourself may bring a surprising result. There are those who find that, having listened to their intuition, they do not to use crystals or they feel they cannot assist people. They may be sensitive and find the crystal energy too much or they may not trust what they feel. If you don't want to do anything, or your intuition says keep away then that is your right, you do not have to assist if you do not feel happy about it. If you find the energy from the crystals to be too strong then it is possible to train and learn to utilize that ability in other ways. There are those who say they cannot feel anything, this may be because they are not allowing themselves the space to feel the energies of either people or crystals. Others say they do not have the skills to help people. Recognizing that limitation is good. If they want to help then there are lots of different courses available at all different levels of ability. Many are run in a way where past experience is not necessarily considered. Everyone has, if they are physically and mentally fit, some ability to be a healer. The degree of ability depends on the innate gifts, self-belief and practice.

# A BRIEF HISTORY OF CRYSTAL HEALING

There does not seem to be a concise history to crystal healing. It would appear that the use of crystals in a healing environment has been going on for a very long time. There are legends about Atlantis and other lands that have long since vanished. Much of this information has come through channelled sources. Channelled information comes through ordinary people who appear to have a connection with either individual spirits or a good affiliation to the universal energy or whatever you believe to be a greater power. The source of their information does not invalidate them, but it can be difficult to differentiate which information relates to what timespan and place. However, much of this information does relate to the use of crystals in many ways. They would appear to have been used to generate power, to assist in communicating over great distances and in healing, with hospital-like environments made from crystals. Most libraries and New Age specialist bookshops have books on the legends of Atlantis and other places. Many cultures that still have remnants of their histories remaining, including Native American, Aborigine and Maori, still use crystals, particularly clear quartz as objects of power, mystery and healing, as they have for many thousands of years. The healers and Medicine People may carry crystals for their own use, use them on other people or even grind them up for their patients to take internally. Many of the training rituals from tribes around the world use crystals as a symbol for new life or for light and energy.

Crystals have also been used in the, so-called, civilized world by kings, queens, rulers and religious leaders as a sign of wealth and power. The jewellery of state: crowns, breastplates and other symbols of their power are set with gemstones. Why? Yes they look nice, yes they stand out in a crowd, yes they may have value, but maybe there is a deeper reason. That reason has probably been lost, or if not it is a well-kept secret; it could be that certain stones and certain combinations of crystals and gemstones help with a leader's

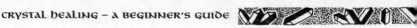

power, to help leaders increase their natural abilities of intuition, psychic powers, protection and control of people? We hear of the *crown* being fought over, not the *ruler*; it is the *ring* that signifies the Bishop, not the *person*; and even today there are coronations where the monarch is presented with a crown and other symbols covered in gemstones and crystals.

Over time powers and values have been attributed to crystals in many different societies and over the last few years more healers have been accessing that information, utilizing it and passing it on. They have found that certain stones have certain effects and certain benefits when used in crystal healing. In general, there have been similarities about the meaning of these attributes from different people; the attributes found in most books tend to agree although, of course, there are occasional differences. In communications with crystal healers around the world, there are basic agreements about the purpose of many stones but occasionally there are big differences about the use of particular stone. All you can do in these situations is follow your own feelings and findings. Crystal healing has grown in popularity and, at the time of writing this book, there are many crystal healers and schools teaching crystal healing. It is recognized by the various organizations that have been set up to monitor and police complementary medicine. Many Natural Healing Centres have crystal healers working at them and many other types of complementary therapists are adding crystal healing to their work.

# ῠOW TO USE TῌIS ΒOOK

This book is designed for those who are just starting on their new path of crystal healing. This may be your first look at any complementary therapy or anything called alternative or you may have already tried several others; if you have you may find that you already know about some of the items mentioned, please bear with this as we all had to start somewhere. It was also written for those who have no crystals, so there is detailed advice about choosing crystals. Crystal healing is not a linear process but books, by nature,

are. Therefore, it is important to work through the book, but you may want to read Chapter 4 next and then return to Chapter 2. Don't forget to read Chapter 4 again after Chapter 3 as they are all related. You may feel that it takes a long time to reach the position of using crystals, this is true, but the preparations are in some ways just as important as the use of crystals.

There are exercises at the end of each chapter. Some are a guide to the information provided in the chapter, others are separate and may require additional work. They are all an integral part of the learning process and of using crystal healing. Many are there to help develop your own skills.

I hope you enjoy using this book and that you find the use of crystals to be stimulating as well as satisfying.

Note that the terms *person*, *client* and *other person* are used interchangeably. The terms *negative* and *positive* energy relate to the state of energy in a body system, with negative being out of balance or unbalancing, and positive being in balance and balancing.

## PRACTICE

The first exercise is to read the book right through before picking up a single crystal. The second is to start to keep a record of various things that happen to you. For instance if you notice that you have performed an intuitive act, such as knowing who was telephoning you, then write it down. Also, note in this record any changes in your self that you experience as you work through the book. So some form of exercise book or journal book will come in useful.

# how to choose, cleanse and care for crystals

*Although it would be exciting just to start crystal healing on someone by holding a crystal and waving it about it is not the best way of helping anyone. Various things have to be done first. These include preparing the crystals, cleansing them after use and creating the best atmosphere in which to work. If you have not got any crystals, read this chapter before going out to buy a collection. Later there is a section on which crystals will be needed for use with the exercises in this book. Some of the work in this chapter takes a little while to get used to, so, if you find that nothing happens, do not worry or panic. Also don't try too hard, relax and have another go. It will come to you when you least expect it. Don't forget to write down your experiences.*

## Choosing

Although you may read about these topics in nearly every book on crystal healing, it is an important subject. It is one of the main parts of learning to listen to crystals. Trying to work with crystals that are not right for you or are dirty or weak will produce poor results at best and be dangerous to all involved at worst. In some senses, it would be like trying to make a gourmet meal from the contents of a dustbin without looking at what you were doing. Therefore, using our kitchen table approach, it is not necessary to go on long journeys in the mountains to find each crystal or for it to come from a guru living in a cave somewhere exotic. Nice as that may seem, it is easier for us to go to a shop which sells crystals for healing or, if necessary, purchase by mail order from a company used to helping

people select crystals; some will choose them for you on an individual basis. As these services vary, try looking in one of the New Age magazines for advertizers of services that you feel comfortable with.

## Where do you get your crystals?

Although buying by mail order is not highly recommended, it may be all that is available to you. If so, always send your intent about your needs with your order. Do this in both mind and writing: tell the supplier what the crystals are for and state the size, shape, point size and any other requirements you may have. If necessary draw a little picture and telephone the supplier, before sending your order, to get the prices and so that the supplier also gets to know you a little bit. Most crystal sellers, including those who sell specimens or jewellery, are now recognizing the healing qualities of crystals even if it is just for the benefit of their bank balance! Moreover, they are becoming more accommodating to the needs of the crystal healer.

Many shops sell a few crystals as a sideline. They may not know what they are buying or what they are selling, so it is up to you to make the decision as to what you buy and what it is. There may be an opportunity to buy in quantity. If you see it, like it and the price is right – BUY IT. Tomorrow it may be gone; you will nearly always be able to find someone else to buy some of your excess.

The best place to buy crystals from is a crystal healer or crystal healing training school where the person selling knows about stones and has already selected the best crystals from the wholesaler. Price is important, as you have limited resources; crystals may be esoteric but be realistic and use any opportunities that arise. You may find that as your layouts become more advanced you need more than one or two pieces of each crystal so any quantity purchase may come in useful more quickly than you had anticipated.

Occasionally you will come across the most amazing crystal you have ever seen. If it is for you it may mean going without other crystals or entertainment for a while, but if it is your intuition and not your avarice saying the crystal is waiting for you, think about

buying it. The alternative is to take the view that if it is still there on your return after a set timespan such as 24 hours or next week, then it is yours. It is a difficult balance to reach; listen to your inner voice and make your decision.

## INTUITION

Having located some stones that you think you want to buy, how do you choose which ones will come home with you? The best way is to use your intuition, but intuition can be a fickle being and not be there when you need it most. Why does it seem to vanish when you think you most need it?

Probably because of stress, strain and trying too hard, so attempt to relax, not always easy in a busy or strange shop with others watching you. Take three good deep breaths and let them out as noisily and with as much release as circumstances permit. Close your eyes for a few moments and ground yourself. Let roots grow out of your feet on every out breath and then suck grounding energy up through these roots on every in breath; see Chapter 4 for the full exercise. Now let your intuition in; don't try, just let it come into your mind like trying to see something on the edge of your vision. Listen to the little voice inside you; talk with it, ask it which stones are for you today. Which crystals are the right ones to take home with you.

Ask the crystals to be placed on the counter so that you can use the following methods. Most shops will oblige and, if they don't, consider taking your custom elsewhere. Try to ignore the assistant's beady eye; remember every customer may be a shoplifter.

## FEELING WITH THE HAND

You may prefer to add some action to enhance your intuitive process, so you can stop being a closet intuit and wave your arms around. Carefully place your hand, palm down, about 10 to 15 cm

(4 to 6 inches) above the stones under consideration. Again, relax as deeply as possible, block out as much of what is going on around you as you can and note what sensations you can now feel. BELIEVE in what you feel. That tingling, feeling of heat, or cold, or strange sensation in your hand is not your imagination; you are picking up the energy of the crystals. Ask, 'Which stones are for me?', or 'Which stones want to help me in my work?' If the situation allows, place the stones individually on the counter, feel over them

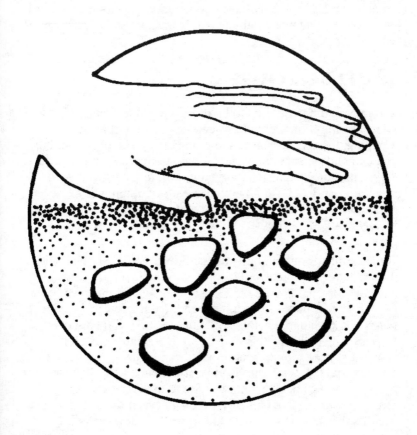

**Figure 2**  Choosing with a hand

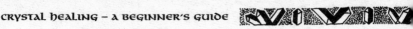

with your hand, and ask each one if it is for you. See what answers you get. You may want to practise this at home with pebbles or other objects before venturing into a shop.

This process can be enhanced by the use of a pendulum. Pendulums are a great joy and a great help. They do require one important thing – good questions. Woolly or generalized questions do not work. If you can spread the crystals out, you can ask the pendulum to answer 'yes' or 'no' to the question 'Do you want to work with me?' If you only have enough money for one crystal ask, 'Which crystal will work with me?' or 'Which crystal should I buy? Please show yes.'

# Pendulums

You may find a pendulum to be of help when learning to trust your own intuition. Pendulums can be made from almost anything: the classic is a wedding ring on a piece of cotton, but you can choose something else. Although this is a little like the 'chicken-and-egg' question you may want to choose a crystal pendulum and you will have to use your intuition, not a pendulum. There are also wooden and lead glass pendulums readily available. Whether it has string, cord or chain is a personal choice.

To use your pendulum, hang the cord over your first finger with the weight on the outside. Place your thumb over the cord allowing between 8 to 12 cm (3 to 5 inches) to hang down to the weight. Now it needs to be initialized; hold it a few inches above your right knee and ask the pendulum to show you your symbol for YES. The first time this may take a few minutes to get a result, just keep the question in your mind. Having found the yes symbol hold the pendulum over your left knee and ask it for your NO symbol. Again, give yourself time to make the connection. The third symbol that can be useful is between the knees and is the ZERO POINT, the 'I don't know' or no action symbol. This is a brief outline of how to use a pendulum; the best thing to do is practise at home before venturing out, remembering to use questions that give yes/no answers (see Figure 11 in Chapter 4).

## Jumping crystals

Sometimes a crystal will just jump out at you, it will appear to be bright and sparkling; no one else may have noticed it. You may even see it move, forcing its way into your vision. If in doubt turn away and look back and, if it is still on top shining like the pole star – go for it. This is a good response, but if no crystals jump out at you do not worry, your crystal may not have been there, or you were trying too hard.

## Ask it!

This method may seem a little strange the first few times you try it! In your mind, or out loud if possible, talk to the displayed crystals. Ask them if they are for you. Ask how they can help you. Beware, the response may not be what you were expecting. It may not be for working with other people: it may be for work on you, for meditating with or to place in your sitting room, bedroom or workspace. To a certain extent, you may go out to buy a stone for a specific purpose, but do not be too single-minded. Let your intuition go with the flow. If you are not having much luck choosing a stone, try to stay relaxed. Repeat your breathing exercise of three really good deep breaths and change the question so that it is applied to each individual crystal 'will you help me in any way'. See what response you get. If there is a positive answer you can buy the stone and when you get it home clean and charge it and then ask it further questions about how the two of you are going to work together. You should always be polite when talking to the stones, say 'please' and 'thank you' and do not take them for granted. When you have chosen and cleansed the stone, meditate with it. This will help you to discover the relationship between you and the stone.

One final comment, when choosing naturally pointed crystals such as clear quartz, amethyst, citrine or smoky quartz, try to choose those with undamaged points. As you will find out later, one of the sources of energy of the crystal is this main termination. Any damage may affect the energy release of the crystal.

So you have purchased your crystal and have taken it home. You now have to make it feel welcome.

# CLEANSING

Throughout history, there have been examples of acts of welcome to houses, caves and tents. Often this included some form of cleansing with water, smoke or oils either in actuality or in a symbolic form. These acts of cleansing are symbols of love or respect even in our modern times.

The giving of perfume, running the bath for a loved one, sharing a bath, making the room smell nice when expecting company and the splashing on of after-shave by adolescents are all messages of welcome and cleansing. This is what you need to do for your crystals. Welcome them into your home and cleanse them, feed them, and care for them.

## The controversy

There is controversy about the use of salt water: that is water, often spring or well water, that has salt, normally sea salt added to it to form a saline solution. This has been the main way of cleansing for quartz and other impervious stones for a long time.

Current views indicate that this is not a good idea, that it damages the matrix or energy structure of the crystal. So, please bear that in mind. However, dunking suitable crystals in salt water and rinsing them off in clean water does work well. It is not like soaking them for a long time – a short shower instead of a long soak produces fewer wrinkles!

Some crystals do not like water at all. It will damage them. A prime example is Turquoise; some others do not like salt water or salt. So great care has to be taken. The softer and more pervious the crystal the less physical the cleansing process can be.

The following list of cleansing methods gives a broad outline of the different methods available.

## Salt

Suitable crystals can be placed in sea salt to cleanse them. This is a powerful method of cleansing. Use it only on strong stones. Depending on how much cleansing needs to take place determines the time the stone remains in the salt. The idea is to bury the stone in the salt. Place a layer of salt in a glass bowl, place the stone in the middle of the salt and add more salt on top of the crystal. Remember that by its nature salt pulls water out of everything that surrounds it. Therefore, it will take water from a stone and from the surrounding atmosphere so that on a humid day you could end up with sludge and possibly a damaged crystal. Salt is good for crystals used in deep healing that then need to be thoroughly cleansed.

## Water cleansing

Again, this method is not for all crystals. Clear running streams are best; but from the kitchen-table approach, the water from the cold tap makes a second best. Remember to keep your mind on cleansing the crystal, to remove all of its negative energy and for the neutralization of that negative energy. Some crystals can also be rinsed in a bowl of fresh water after salt water cleansing. Beware of leaving stones in running water, as they also like to run and may disappear. If you live near a sacred well, or visit one on holiday, you may be able to collect a few containers of the well water and use it to cleanse or rinse your crystals.

## Earth cleansing

The earth is a powerful healer and a powerful transposer of energies. A crystal that has worked hard and lost all of its lustre and vitality may benefit from being buried in the soil. Be careful to mark the spot well. Crystals may want to return to Mother Earth for good! One safe way is to use a clay flower pot, part fill it with earth and

place your crystal in the pot, fill the pot with more earth and bury this in the ground, marking it with a large sign! These stones may have been working with people who have had a very serious illness or those approaching death. These stones need a long time, maybe several months or even more to rest, be cleansed and recharged. When you think they may be ready ask them and, if they agree, dig them up and rinse them in flowing water.

## Smudge

Smudge is one of my favourite words and things to do. Smudge is a mix of herbs and to use them you set light to them and use the smoke as a cleansing material. You can smudge yourself, the cat, rooms, crystals and some children. Smudging, used worldwide, is a very ancient ceremony.

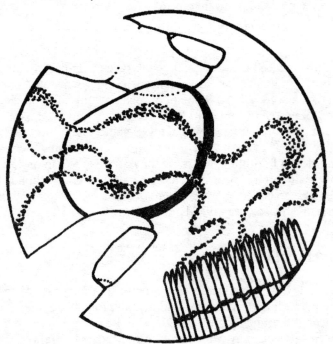

**Figure 3** Smudge with burning herbs

You can buy smudge in two basic forms. The first, and in some ways most convenient, is as a stick. This is a bundle of herbs bound by string. The second is as a loose mixture that you put in a fireproof bowl (a clay pot or shell). Smudge is available from many shops, by mail order from shamanic suppliers or, for relaxation and fun, you can also make your own. The herbs most commonly used are sage, cedar and lavender.

The sage can be red or white, from your garden, the supermarket or from the plains of Mexico. The cedar is harder to find but there are cedar trees on older estate gardens. Various cedars have been used including *Juniperus virginia* and *Thuja occidentalis*. Walk around after a windy day and pick up a few bits. The lavender can come from anywhere. In addition, you can use Sweetgrass, Mugwort and Lady's Bedstraw.

Do not use essential oils instead, as they are too strong and in some cases can be dangerous. Beware – burning smudge may set off your smoke alarm.

To cleanse crystals light your smudge stick and let it smoulder, fanning it with a feather or rolled-up newspaper. Hold the crystal in the smoke for a few minutes and that is it. Remember your intent for the negative energies to be removed and transformed. If you are burning loose smudge, place it in a fireproof dish or large shell; use a match to light it. Sometimes, it takes several matches to get it going. Fan the smoke from the smouldering mixture over your crystals.

Try smudging the room after an argument and particularly after a crystal healing session. Feel the difference and relax into that feeling. It is a nice procedure to smudge the room after the physical cleansing of dusting and vacuuming, waft the smudge smoke into the corners, towards the ceiling and floor and feel the difference.

The scientific background to smudging is worth mentioning here. We live in a time of monumental scientific change where everything is new and exciting, never been done before, and we can't keep up with it. It's out of date before it's out of the box.

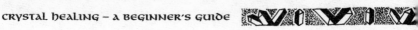

Well, slow down and realize that it has been done before. The electronics industry relies on quartz and other crystals for its existence, but is their use new? Not according to history. Your watch, television, cooker, computer, car and nearly everything else has a piece of quartz or silicon, one of quartz's basic elements, in it. And so it is with smudging – not the quartz, but ions. Although people did not understand the theory they knew that burning certain plants helped clear away negative energy. Ions are electrically charged molecules that carry extra energy.

Bad energy ions are called positive ions and good energy ions are called negative ions. So named to confuse us or so it seems. When you stand by a waterfall the air feels and smells good, you may feel energized and possibly light headed. This is because the action of the waterfall is releasing negative ions, (they're the good ones) and taking away positive ions, (they're the bad ones). The same happens after a thunderstorm; the positive ions cause that heavy headachy feeling before a storm. When the storm breaks, the falling rain brings negative ions into existence, which clear away the positive ions and cleanse the air leaving a feeling of freshness.

With smudging, the herbs burnt for thousands of years help dispose of positive ions and generate negative ions, bringing energies into balance. Taking this one stage further, after the question of 'so what has this to do with crystals' comes the fact the using crystals in healing may change their ion balance. The crystal absorbs the positive ions and releases the negative ions. Thus, the crystal needs cleansing to remove the bad ions and let the crystal regain its balance and natural ion structure. Smudging, washing in salt water, holding in running water or burying in the earth does just this.

One of the nicest things to smudge is your friends, yourselves and the room you are in. Not recommended in the middle of a drinking session, but it does help to reduce stress, old atmospheres and, maybe, the need to drink in the first place.

Well, all this smudging should have got your crystals to a point of absolute cleanliness, now they need to regain some energy.

# Charging

Like us, crystals need to be fed. Their food is the energy of nature and includes the sun, moon and running water. Again a little warning, some stones lose their colour in strong sunlight. So, do not leave coloured stones out in the garden or on the windowsill all summer; a short period is quite safe.

## Sun, moon and thunderstorms

Place the cleansed stone on a sunny or moon-filled windowsill or outside on a wall. Remember that crystals are attractive to all sorts of beings, so keep them secluded and away from whomsoever or what ever. The type of energy used to charge your crystals is up to you and the stone: you can always ask it. In most cases 24 hours is enough, but in cloudy weather, they may require a little longer. A mix of energies is fine; I charge my stones in all weathers, sun, moon, cloud and rain. This should provide a balanced diet. Again, it is the intent that is important, in this case to provide the crystals with their natural energy. Many women like to use the moon's rays to charge their crystals as it has a strong connection with female energy, healing and intuition.

Before leaving them out in a thunderstorm consider the release of energy that occurs. You may feel that it is an important energy, so go for it. Remember that they need to be safe. Outside in a storm the heavy rain may help them to return to their birthplace by washing them away.

## Streams

Charging crystals by streams can be a gentle method of feeding them. You can build a little sacred space or sanctuary by, or even over, the stream to place the stones on. Where possible it is nice if it is a secluded place, both for you and the stones. Other people in close proximity to the stones may change their energy field. Again 24 hours is a guide time; ask the stones if they feel charged or use your intuition by looking at their energy and appearance.

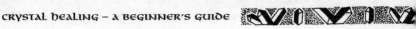

# Personal power

For cleansing and charging, it is possible to use your own breath. To do this centre and ground yourself, still your mind as much as possible and concentrate on the crystal. Breathe on it and focus on removing any negative energy held in the crystal. When you feel you have accomplished this, breathe on it again with the intent of adding good healing energy to feed the crystal.

This is a useful process when faced with a situation where the other methods are not available or when there is insufficient time for full cleansing. So now, in one way or another and after a little time, your crystals are ready to work. How do you look after them until you are ready to use them?

# Caring

Be nice to your crystals. Having chosen, cleansed and charged your crystals, you still have to care for them. Like many things, crystals like to be nurtured, loved and utilized for their given purpose. Placing them away from light, warmth and company is the worst thing to do. Crystals are survivors; they have been around for a very long time! They like to be close to people and people like to be close to crystals. However, there is a balance. Fill your rooms full of crystals and you may become over-energized by the crystals. A few stones around us can be good. Several hundred crystals in the bedroom may cause sleepless nights or strange dreams.

Place them in attractive containers, cover them with material to keep the dust off and burn incense or, of course, smudge to keep the air fresh and energized. This, of course, helps the crystals and keeps your room feeling pleasant. Talk to crystals or communicate with them. Pick them up, feel them and sit with them. Even a few moments in a day with a crystal can turn that day around into something special.

# Talk and Listen to Them

This is an important part of finding out how the crystal manifests its energies and how it can help you and your work with crystals. Sit quietly and relax, centre yourself, feel your energy coming from the locality of your navel. Allow yourself to dwell in that area. Pick up your crystal and place it in your left hand, feel and touch it. Look at it, hold it up to the light, think about what makes it different from all the other crystals; find rainbows, reflections and refractions, enjoy the brilliance of the stone.

Close your eyes, keep the crystal in your left hand, hold it up to your heart, and start to tune in to your crystal. Let your mind go as quiet and blank as you can. It is hard to stop the internal chatter, try to let it pass into the background. Keep an image of your crystal in your mind's eye. Say hello; ask it questions about the power it possesses and how it can help in your crystal healing. Again, trust what happens. Think of it this way, if it is your imagination, then you seem to have a large knowledge about this crystal, so does it matter whether it is imagination or not.

If you get a complete blank, do not get upset or concerned. It can take several attempts to get a clear connection, it is similar to tuning in an old-fashioned television or radio and it takes a little time. You have to get the right frequency. The worst thing to do is to panic; instead put the stone down and try again a little while later and remember to relax as much as possible. It may be helpful to play a tape of gentle relaxing music to mask other activities going on around you.

# Natural fibres, but remember the kitchen table

It is good to use beautiful and natural items to keep your crystals in and cover your crystals with. However, take the pragmatic approach and use what you have around you. Slowly build up your collection of containers, cloths and storage space. Remember not to turn

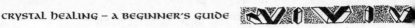

crystals into gods and goddesses; they have survived in the ground, been extracted, transported and bought and sold, to help you and your work. Treat them fairly and carefully and they will be your allies for a long time.

Place them somewhere you can see them on a regular basis. However, be warned – as your collection grows so does the need for storage space so you may have to move them to a different part of the room or even a different room.

Meanwhile, you can now choose, cleanse, charge and look after your crystals. As you read through this book you can sit with your crystal in your hand – learning together! The question that you may still be asking is 'What is the first crystal I should buy?' This is dealt with in Chapter 3, but I would recommend a clear quartz point about 5 cm (2 inches) long and as clear as you can afford. Enjoy each other's company.

## pRActice

There is a lot to do in this practice session. As a suggestion, it may be a good idea to spend several days working through this part.

This is where you have to go out and buy some crystals, maybe one or two at a time so that you can come home and practise your choosing techniques again. However, if the crystal shop is a long way away or you are buying by mail order you may have to buy several in one go. Look ahead to Chapter 3 and the section on the minimum set of crystals to help you decide what to purchase. If you need to, you can probably get smudge sticks at the same time. If you already have sufficient crystals, try the various methods of choosing with the crystals you have. Put them all together and ask which one would be good for you today, use your hands, vision and intuition.

When you get your crystals, you will need to cleanse them. Try several of the methods described and see which you prefer. All the methods are safe for the given set but in future beware of putting all crystals in salt, water or salt water.

Next charge the crystals, try several methods to see which ones you like. This is, of course, weather dependent, if there is a lot of cloud leave them out anyway. See if you can feel any difference after 24 hours. You can always change your methods as you learn.

Find somewhere attractive to store your precious crystals, such as a basket or box. Decide whether you want them to see light, be in the dark, or covered with a cloth. Spend some time being with them; look at them, feel them and just be.

At the end of these exercises, you should have a greater feeling for your crystals.

# what is
# crystal healing?

*Crystal healing is not magic or an occult activity. It uses vibrational energy, which works at levels that are not currently accepted by a majority of so-called civilized societies. There are many explanations of how crystal healing works. In this book, there will be several ideas put forward that may be part or all of the explanation; only time will tell. Crystal healing possibly works at vibrational frequencies far higher than those of sound, light or radio waves. A frequency is the number of vibrations in a given timespan, normally measured in vibrations per second. Crystal healing may also work at the very smallest of levels, the sub-atomic level where the particles are very small. Crystal healing may also work because of the idea that people can heal themselves and that the healer is only acting as a catalyst or guide. The healer does not heal. This may all seem strange when compared with orthodox medicine where the intervention of the doctor and surgeon is considered as necessary. There are, of course, times when this form of external intervention is indeed life saving. There would seem to be a place and need for all sorts of help for those that are unwell.*

Crystal healing is part intuition, part fact. The skill is bringing these two together in a safe and effective way. The intuitive part is in deciding what to do, how to use the crystals and which crystals to use. The intuition may be assisted by or even based on a good background of knowledge, the fact; but in the end, it is the intuitive process that is crucial. Although there are many theories about crystal healing, the final reality is that it works for some people, for some problems, some of the time. More evidence is being produced to help show how healing works. Science is changing; people like Albert Einstein have broadened the path of knowledge and enabled

society to remove some of the blinkers that have stopped the acceptance of new things.

# Energy and vibration

This section has a technical aspect, so try not to be put off by this as it may just help with your understanding of the subject. Modern physics says that all matter is made from energy and that all energy is a form of vibration. In addition, when matter, which is made from energy, is magnified it appears to be made up of a very large proportion of nothing, of space, the solid parts form only a very small part of the whole. There are lots of different forms of vibrations, examples include sound, a mechanically made vibration that works a mechanical device in the ears to transduce or change the energy into an impulse that our brain tells us is a voice or music. Another vibration is radio or television signals, whether they are on medium wave or from a satellite, they are specific vibrations that are caught by the aerial, or satellite dish, changed into visual or audio vibrations and again we pick them up through our eyes and ears.

As people are no different from any other form of matter, it is possible to relate this concept as one idea about how people work. When people are fit, well and happy, the components that they are made from, their matter which is made up from energy which is a vibration, vibrate at a given rate, a happy, healthy rate. The different parts may vibrate at different rates depending on their structure, with each structure having a happy, healthy rate of vibration. However, when the body becomes unwell the structure changes, different proportions of chemicals are working in the body and in extreme situations the actual physical structure may change.

This change in components or structure is also a change in vibration. It is like changing channel on the television, in that you get a different picture from a different vibration, the vibration being the information sent from the channel provider. Therefore, for the human being the rate of vibration has changed. This may be for one small part of the body system but if that is not treated, the changed

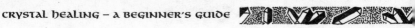

vibration may influence other parts as well. To bring the body back to a state of wellness the vibrational rate needs to be returned to the original rate or a new healthy and happy rate.

# VIBRATIONAL MEDICINE

A way of changing the vibrational rate to the healthy, happy rate is vibrational medicine, which uses another vibrating substance to change the rate of vibration in the body. One vibrational medicine is crystal healing. So how can one vibrating substance change the rate of vibration or frequency of another vibrating substance? One answer is to apply the Theory of Resonance. There are many examples of resonance, the most common are to do with pianos and clocks. It is known that if several pianos are placed close to each other and a particular note is struck, the same note on the other pianos will sound quietly. What happens is the string that has been struck vibrates; that vibration is of a specified frequency. As it travels through the air or other material and meets all the other strings it finds a friend in the one of exactly the same length or note and where its vibrational rate fits exactly. Other close fitting notes exist, these are the same note, but in different octaves, this is because there is a precise relationship between notes in different octaves.

The example of clocks can produce a similar result. For this experiment you need several traditional pendulum clocks all hung on the same wall. If you were to set them all going you would notice that all the pendulums were swinging at different rates. After a few days, the pendulums would all be swinging together at the same rate. The vibrations of the clocks, the swings of the pendulum will have resonated with each other. Each pendulum affects the other, a vibration, so that they gradually move into alignment.

The piano can be heard and the clocks can be seen. However, with vibrational medicine, neither the healing vibrations, nor the vibrations in the body can be seen, so what happens remains a mystery. However, modern science tells us that at the minute level,

the sub-atomic level, there are still vibrations and as all matter is actually made from vibrations, this can then be applied to the body and the substances used in vibrational medicine. The vibrational rate is far higher, the objects are far smaller, but the principle remains the same. The important factor is to get the correct vibration for the particular imbalance. It is hoped that the good resonance is stronger than the diseased resonance. Maybe this is why it is harder to treat problems that have existed for a long time or those that have deeply invaded the body or mind. Their resonance may be stronger than the vibration of the substance being used in the treatment.

This is only one idea but one that seems to fit the practical facts; time may well prove it one way or the other. It does show that the healing works at a very small level, the sub atomic level where only a small amount of energy will be required to make changes and that the energy transmitted or transmuted by crystals may be strong compared to that which is being changed.

To this can be added that crystals do act as transducers, a substance that actually changes one form of energy into another. For example, by hitting clear quartz, mechanical energy, the crystal will produce electricity, another form of energy. If you assume that there is a universal energy, referred to in many ancient texts as *chi*, *prana* and *ki*, all around us then the crystal and the healer may transduce that energy into a form that will help with healing.

# Colour healing

Another way of looking at crystal healing, still from the idea of vibrational medicine, is as an extension of colour healing. Some crystal healers do use the colour of the stones as a guide, taking one of the views of the colour of the *chakras* as the starting point. Any particular colour is the part of light that is reflected back to the eye; the coloured object absorbs the rest. When an object appears to be yellow it is reflecting the light of a vibrational frequency that responds to yellow and absorbing the rest of the visible spectrum. So, is it the other colours that have an effect?

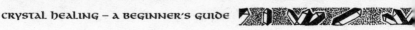

When a person is in the area of a colour the frequency or vibrations are of a very specific nature due to the colour. These vibrations are not as high as crystal vibrations, being in the visible spectrum, but they are still a vibrational medicine. Consider the colour of the items around us, the colour of rooms or clothes, and how they affect how we feel; for instance, red for anger and pale green for calmness. Colour has a strong influence in our language and is particularly connected to the emotions and feelings: green with envy, yellow with jealousy, in a black mood, or red with anger. Colour also plays an important part in 'power dressing', creating an impression by our surroundings. Although there are differences in different cultures, there is always a strong relationship between colour and feelings. Therefore, crystals may be working on more than one level of vibration at the same time, as their inherent vibration is far higher than the visible spectrum vibration. They may also be working at more than one level of the person with the different levels of vibration affecting either different parts of the structure or affecting atomic or sub-atomic particles in different ways.

# Space

Another important contributing factor as to why crystal healing works is the space it provides for the individual. In these days of mass communication, travel, work, television, telephones and a hectic lifestyle, there is rarely any space to really relax, really rest, really let the body and mind sort out what is going on. We watch television to relax but, because of the nature of programmes with violence and tension and by not taking into account the effect of the emissions of electromagnetic vibrations, it causes stress. We have a drink to relax, which again has detrimental effects on our chemical and emotional balance. We go for a drive in the country, but there is still a car in front of us, or sit on the beach along with millions of other people, so we are still interacting and under stress. We read a book, but it is not relaxing or stress free because we are either trying to learn or being driven by the story.

The time taken for crystal healing helps to provide a special relaxing space, normally in a reasonably quiet and calm environment: no telephone and nowhere to go, with a chance to talk and express emotions. Part of the treatment may involve a relaxation exercise and counselling, both of which are just for the client. No one else has to be considered, no one else can hear and in the professional situation, it is entirely confidential. It is a wonderfully selfish time; a time that rarely materializes elsewhere these days. Therefore, an hour for the individual may also have the beneficial effect of being the only true time for relaxation, release and self. Allowing the body to start healing itself.

This has been a brief explanation of some of the ways that crystal healing may work and assist in the general improvement of the well being of the individual. As yet, there is no scientifically accepted version, but the time for that is getting closer.

# What crystals will I need?

Although you will not be using any crystals in this chapter, it is important look at what crystals you will need when you start to use them. Unfortunately these are not normally available from the kitchen and have to be purchased from a suitable outlet. Sometimes you may be given the right stone at the right time, if so, lucky you! The first stones you will use are single clear quartz terminated crystals; or in plain English, a clear pointy one. To help you identify this crystal, one of the most common of crystals, it normally has six sides and may be clear all the way through or cloudy from the bottom for some or all of its length. They may just be labelled as quartz, quartz points, clear quartz, or some other combination. They come in many shapes, sizes and clarity. The surface can also be very bright or quite dull.

What is under consideration is a natural stone, there are polished samples on the market that are very effective but they cost more and at this stage it is important to use the natural stone to obtain as much information about the stone as possible. Try to find one that

has a good undamaged point, regular faces and triangles. The crystal needs to be between 3 and 6 cm (1.5 and 2.5 inches) long. If you find one that is smaller or bigger and it is right for you then fine, remember that we are trying not to have rules. See Chapter 2 for how to choose your crystals and, as stated in the Introduction, this book is linear but the process is not or in this case the other way round. You will need two clear quartz points of similar shape and size, referred to as a pair, and if you can find them together that will be really good as they may have come from the same place or even grown up together.

**Figure 4** Minimum set of crystals

# What is a pair of crystals?

The idea of a pair of crystals is that they are two similar stones in shape, size and energy. The size and layout of the sides, triangles and points should be similar, there may be different impurities in each stone. The way they feel should be very similar, with similar energies. There are also pairs that seem to have different but complementary energies such as male and female stones. It is also possible to build similar pairs into larger sets of a dozen or more stones.

You will also need a chakra set; these are a set of tumbled or polished crystals, each about 2.5 cm (1 inch) in diameter, see Figure 4. There are several versions of chakra sets made from different crystals; each has its own merits and uses. You may be able to buy a ready made set, but it is far more fun to practise and use your skills to select each stone yourself. This particular chakra set has been selected as a good basic starting point. You can add different stones as you learn about their merits. The stones you need are amethyst, sodalite, blue lace agate, rose quartz, citrine, carnelian and hematite. This will then give you the basic working set, one for each major chakra.

There are several views about the use of rough or polished stones. As a starting point polished or tumbled stones are probably more easily available. They also show their colour and patterns more clearly making visual identification easier. Rough or unpolished crystals are not as easy to come by and can be harder to identify visually. The choice is very much personal preference and availability. Finding natural pieces of crystals is not always possible, but if you can find what you want that is excellent.

There are a few other stones that you may find useful. First, two or three pieces of rose quartz will be helpful. Polished or tumbled are better for here as the natural pieces can be razor sharp and will cut hands easily. They need to be large enough to hold in the hands easily, between the size of a walnut and a small orange. A couple of pieces of hematite can also be useful, again the size needs to be about that of a walnut, although hematite tends to be on the flat

side. Two pieces of aventurine, a green sparkling stone, of a size to hold in the hands will also come in useful but are not essential.

Before rushing out to buy these refer to the section on choosing stones in Chapter 2.

# Do we really need crystals?

This may seem a strange paragraph to have in a book about crystal healing but you may read or be told by people that you do not need crystals to heal. This may or may not be true; however, something has brought you to the decision that you want to try them. They do have unique properties but over a period, you may use fewer crystals and more healing energy. Remember that crystals bring their own energy to the situation, just as the healer brings their energy and ability to help the other person change themselves. This is fine as long as you do not deplete your own energy levels; there are sections later in the book that guide you through protection exercises. There are many types of healing, some healers prefer some types of healing; some people prefer a particular type of complementary therapy and then a change occurs for them and they move on to another form. Some treatments work for some people some of the time. So again, let your intuition assist you in what you are doing. Nevertheless, carry on using crystals whilst you feel that is the correct path to take.

## PRACTICE

This has been a theoretical chapter so the exercises are a little different.

First, make a comfortable space in your room and lie down for 20 minutes. Just let your mind wander or go blank. Maybe think of a beach, very quiet and warm where you feel at peace. Let the warm breeze carry away your concerns and worries. Let the lapping of the waves calm your body and mind. Feel at peace in the warm sun or under the trees in the dappled sunlight. If you are worried about falling asleep set the alarm clock. Remember this is your space, there is nothing else you can do, nowhere else to go. What happened, what did it feel like? This is part of crystal healing, having to take time out.

The second exercise is working with colour. Collect some objects from around the house, all different but bright colours: if possible, at least red, orange, yellow, pink, blue and green. Put them in front of you. Which colour (try to ignore the significance of the object) do you like best? Space the objects so that you can pass your hand over each one without interference from the next and close your eyes. Can you feel any difference? How do they make you feel? Write down your results in your record book.

# ḣANÒLING AND STORING CRYSTALS

Crystals are objects of power, which is why they are used in healing. As such, they need to be cared for and treated with respect. They emit, transduce and transmute energy and in some respects can be likened to a laser, a laser for higher psychic levels of energetic vibration. There is even a type of quartz crystal called a laser wand, which is used as a powerful psychic cutting tool. Although crystals have different types of energy, it appears that all crystals will emit a form of vibrational energy. Because of this, no terminated (pointed – natural or cut) crystal should be waved around in the presence of other people or animals without considering what the effect is going to be. Remember that we have auric layers surrounding us that can be very sensitive to the higher levels of energy. Therefore, all types of crystals should be handled carefully, both for your sake and that of other people around you. At healing festivals, where people should know better, there have been examples of people ducking as a crystal wand has been waved around to cleanse the room; it may cleanse the room but it also cuts into people's auras causing disturbance and unnecessary stress.

Crystals also need respect when they are stored and transported. Be careful of the points, as these are easy to chip and damage. If possible wrap each crystal in a cloth of natural material or have

**Figure 5** Don't wave them around

separate bags for them. Some say that crystals should be wrapped in silk or leather; kitchen paper towel also works well but does not last as long! There is a question of whether crystals should be kept in the dark. One answer to that is that they have come out of the ground, from Mother Earth, and that the darkness is their natural environment. The opposite view is that now they have been born into the light and atmosphere, they should be kept in the light. However, be careful of direct sunlight as that can bleach the colour from some stones. Tumbled and non-terminated natural pieces of crystal also need to be stored carefully, again on natural material in wooden trays or wicker baskets. How you treat or store your stones is up to you, what you feel is best for you and your stones. Sometimes plastic boxes may have to be used, well use what is available at the time.

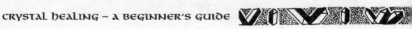

Only use the crystals when you and your intuition says that it is right to do so. Do not use them just because somebody says 'go on, give us a go'. If it doesn't feel right don't do it. You can always say you don't feel up to it or the stones do not feel right. It is your prerogative to say NO, just as you should not force a healing on someone; they have the right to say NO. Listen to your inner self, that little voice. If you do not you could find yourself in a situation that is beyond your scope, which may not do you, or the person being treated any good at all.

Finally, do not hit crystals with hammers. The act of hitting and breaking crystals was well known by ancient societies. So was the amount of energy that could be released. Some may have considered it to be earth shattering. It may not have been the end of the world but the energy released from the shattering crystal could have been enough to kill a person banging the crystal. Crystals hold a lot of energy – when you think of a Piezo gas lighter it is not very big and still produces a reasonable spark, so imagine what a 30 cm (12 inch) crystal would produce! Small crystals produce enough electricity, transformed from mechanical movement, to drive microphones and old record player pickups; these are very small pieces of crystal but with high transducing effects.

Having considered the way we handle and treat crystals it is important to consider the way we act toward the other person and ourselves. We need to treat both with respect, to put ourselves in the best state to assist and to put them in the best state to be assisted. Once learnt these processes will take only a short time to go through each time you work with the crystals.

# Preparation

The first stage of preparation may be to take a bath or a shower to help remove all of the rubbish, both physical and psychic, that has attached itself during the preceding period. In the shower after physically cleansing, try standing away from the shower stream by

30 to 46 cm (12 to 18 inches) and slowly turning around. This can help to physically clean your own aura, the energy layers around your body. The feeling is similar to standing by a waterfall or in breaking waves but more so as there are no clothes in the way. Then dry off and put on clothes in which you feel comfortable working, maybe white as white is a colour of healing and helps to repel negative energy and loose fitting to feel comfortable and not restrict the energy flows. Tight-fitting clothes tend to restrict the flow of energy through the body.

With all healing it is important to be in the here and now not thinking about what you will have for supper or that the grass needs cutting; to reach this state it is essential to be centred and grounded. Before working, you need to allow a little time to relax and to start to remove all of your own problems, from your mind if not in reality. Sit quietly on a chair in the kitchen or dining room, so that your feet are flat on the floor and your back vertical and comfortable. Let your body relax and your mind be calm. If the thoughts keep on coming, then when they come into your mind, imagine them encapsulated in bubbles and let them float gently out of the picture. Let your breathing just take place, don't force it, and feel yourself drop into the present. Place your hands on your lower abdomen so that your navel is in the middle of your hands and feel your body gently moving with each breath. Bring your attention to this area and focus your thoughts upon it, try to breathe down into this area, imagine your breath reaching beyond your lungs to your navel as you breathe in, and starting from your navel and going up as you breath out.

After a few minutes, change your attention to the bottom of your feet where they touch the ground. Feel where they touch the floor, just let your breathing take place, and if your mind wanders let the thoughts go and bring your attention back to your feet. Start to imagine, visualize or see roots growing out of the bottom of your feet, letting them go into the ground; if you are not at ground level imagine your roots going across the floor, down through the walls and then into the ground. With every out-breath feel the roots going deeper and deeper through the soil, clay and rocks that make up the

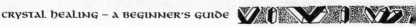

earth's crust. At some stage you will see an orange or golden ball of energy, earth energy, so let your roots go to this. When they do, they may spread out on the surface of the sphere or work their way into the sphere.

At this stage, change your concentration to the in-breath. On every in-breath visualize and, if possible, feel this orange or golden energy come up through your roots, it may move only slowly to start with, and be faint, but after a few attempts it will come into the roots quickly. Let this energy work up to your feet and with every in-breath let it come into your body, into the feet, up past the ankle, into the lower leg, up through the knee into the upper leg. You may feel warmth or tingling as this energy fills your body; it may take several minutes to feel anything. You may feel that you are imagining these sensations, if you do just let them continue and see what happens, and then try it again. Is it still imagination? Let the energy continue its upward journey, into the pelvic region, the lower abdomen filling every organ as it moves up, into the chest area and into the shoulders. Now let it go down your arms into your fingers, back up to your shoulders, into your neck and into your head and face letting it fill your head. Feel your whole body filled with this energy.

Now see this energy coming out of the top of your head like a golden fountain and cascading down around your body, surrounding you with a cocoon of golden orange light. When the flow reaches the ground be sure to see it reabsorbed into the earth, maybe forming puddles like molten gold first and then sinking back into the ground. That completes the earth part of this exercise.

Next see a star above your head and, from that star, see a stream of silver white light coming into the top of your head, in the reverse order to the orange energy, filling your whole body. Remember to feel it go down and then back up your arms, then flowing towards your feet filling your whole body. As it does so see, or feel, the difference in this energy compared to the orange earth energy. When this silver light energy reaches the souls of the feet see this light energy come out of your feet and into the ground. This is an important part, that both energies are seen to go into the ground to complete the circuit. How do you feel now? You should feel both energized and well set on the earth. After the first attempt at this

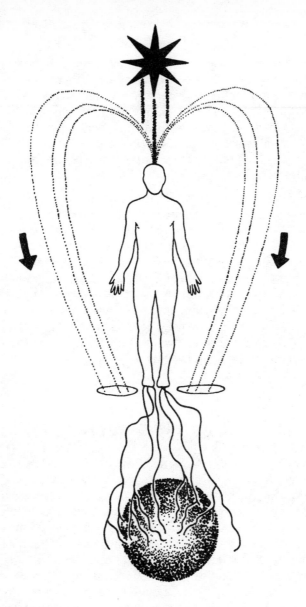

**Figure 6** Grounding

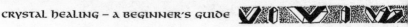

exercise, take a few moments to check through your feelings and body sensations, see whether you feel any changes.

Back to the pre-work checklist. If you have a spirit guide of any sort (as long as they are good ones) then call upon them to assist you, if you have a favourite tree, flower or power animal then ask if their energies will help you. Finally, maintain the cocoon of earth energy around you to act as a barrier between you and other people. If you wish, you could place another barrier of gold or purple light further out than the golden orange layer. This is to stop you absorbing other people's negative energy.

Grounding is important for both the healer and recipient. As well as grounding exercises there are various other ways to help with grounding. Essential oils, crystals, mind games, exercise and food can all help. Which is best depends on the situation and what is available. A sniff of patchouli oil can be helpful for light-headedness. Never put undiluted oils on the skin, and be careful not to sniff too hard! Holding a hematite crystal or even a rock helps with grounding. Smoky quartz and black tourmaline can also help. Jumping up and down or banging your feet on the floor can bring you down to earth. Recalling five facts or reciting a times table backwards brings the mind into the present. A biscuit or two and a cup of tea also can work well.

# Preparing the workspace

Although you can work anywhere, even on the kitchen table, it is good to have a prepared space, one that is relatively clean, tidy and feels good. The less distractions and everyday artefacts around both you and the person you are working with the better. Low level lighting, rather than bright overhead lights, will help to encourage relaxation, but not too low. Gentle calming music in the background is recommended, but beware of sudden noises from the tape or CD player. To start with, the person you are working with needs to have something to lie on. Cushions, a futon or yoga mat should be used together with a pillow for their head and maybe a small cushion under the knees and small of the back.

Having physically cleaned and prepared the space it helps to either smudge the room, burn cleansing and calming essential oils, such as pettigrain or juniper or light a joss stick like rose or cedar. You may also want to ask for the room to be used for the benefit of those who will be working in it. If you do, just sit quietly, relax and ask for just that. Now your space and you are ready. If you have the time just sit in this space and continue keep yourself centred and grounded as you begin to get the feeling of what you are going to do.

You may want to have an altar in this healing space, somewhere to put items that have a spiritual meaning for you. A cloth on a bookcase with photographs, flowers and a candle can be effective.

# feel the energy

The first person's energy you are going to feel is your own. Later you will feel other people's. As you sit in your prepared space feeling relaxed, centred, and grounded, it is a good time to feel energy. To do this gently rub your hands together for 10 to 20 seconds, to activate the nerve endings, then hold your arms out with the palms of your hands facing each other, about 1 metre (3 feet) apart. Relax your hands and arms as much as possible as this helps with your receptive abilities. Slowly bring your hands closer together, letting them bounce gently through the air in very small movements backwards and forwards, an inch at a time and as smoothly as possible. At some stage you may feel, or imagine that you feel a slight resistance, when you do stay with it, bounce your hands gently against this resistance so that the feeling increases. It can be described as pushing gently against a balloon. When you are used to the feeling, which may take several minutes, continue to bring your hands together and you may find another area that gives the same balloon sensation. Practise this several times during the day when you get a quiet moment, it is not essential to be in your prepared space, just nice. It can be difficult to feel these sensations when you are tired or unwell. If there is nothing there do not get concerned; try again in a few minutes or tomorrow. Remember to ground and centre yourself before starting again.

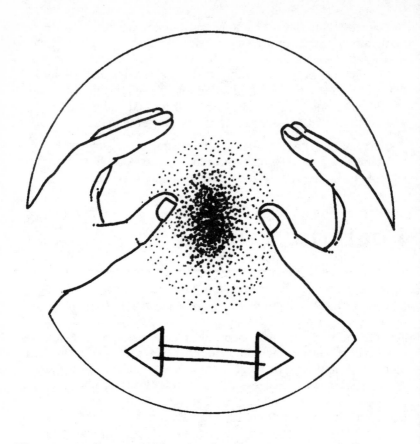

**Figure 7** Feeling energy between hands

What was the balloon feeling? It was part of your own subtle energy system, part of the auric field that surrounds your body. Each different balloon was a different auric layer. When you come to work on other people you will be trying to feel their auric field and subtle energy; these may be perceived in slightly different ways including heat, cold and tingling.

# USING A CRYSTAL

This is it! You are now going to use a crystal, not just on anyone but on yourself. This is the start of training yourself to feel different crystal energies and to find out what effect crystals can have. As a safeguard please read the section below on contra indications, when you have return to here if all is acceptable. You will need to have your clear quartz crystal readily to hand.

If you are starting this as a fresh exercise, you will need to go back and go through the centring and grounding exercises. In this centred state pick up your cleansed and charged clear quartz crystal point, look at it carefully, study it and get to know it. If possible, take your time whilst doing this. Look at any tiny cracks on the surface or inside. Hold your crystal up and notice any rainbows inside as you turn it around. Look at the termination and the other end; see where it was attached to the earth. Gently feel all the surfaces; be careful, as some of them may be sharp. Try holding the crystal in both hands or cuddling it. Remember the feelings you get, write them in your book.

Put the crystal down, if you can. Rub your hands together for 10 to 20 seconds and hold the crystal in your right hand with the point towards your left hand as if you were going to stab your left hand (please don't). Start about 30 cm (12 inches) apart and circle the crystal around in a clockwise direction, then slowly move the crystal towards your left hand. After a while you may begin to feel a little something on your left hand following along the path of the crystal point although it is not touching your left hand. This may be a tingling sensation, a feeling of warmth or cold, or something else. If you don't notice any sensations or you feel that your imagination has run wild, stop, take a couple of relaxing breaths, and gently try again. Do not try too hard!

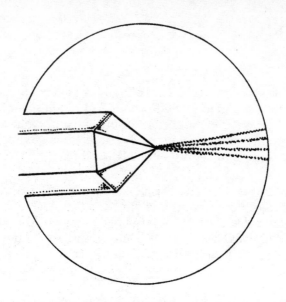

**Figure 8** Energy from crystal point

If you do not feel anything, do not worry, because one day soon you will, accept the situation, enjoy the space and, if you can, try again in 5 minutes or tomorrow. Remember to go through the grounding and centring routine again if you have been doing other things.

If you did feel something keep practising for a while; then you can either carry on or leave the next part for another time, do not push yourself too hard. The next part is to try to feel the different energies from different parts of the crystal. Take the same crystal and hold it so one of the triangular or other shapes that form the point is about 8 cm (3 inches) away from your left hand and paint your hand with it. Use a painting or stroking action working in one direction only, so that on the back stroke you move the crystal up by about 5 cm (2 inches). The movement tends to be circular. Again, you may start to feel something, a tingling, warmth, cold, or some other sensation. Compare this feeling to that of the point and note down the difference.

Finally, in this section use the long side of the crystal, known as the blade, to wipe down your hand about 8 cm (3 inches) away. Keep

repeating this action for a few minutes and record any sensation you get. You have now felt subtle energy from the body, crystal energy from the point, triangle and blade. If you have not managed any or all of these do not worry, just try again another day. This is a very

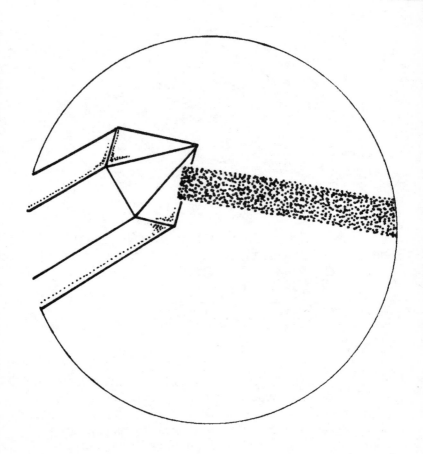

**Figure 9** Energy from triangle

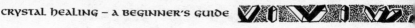

important part of learning about crystals and it is important to get an understanding of this part before moving on.

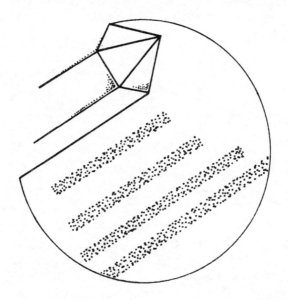

**Figure 10** Energy from blade

# Receiving and sending hands

In the previous section, you used your left hand as the receiving hand, this is common practice, but some people find it better to change this around and use the right hand as the receiving hand. If the energy levels feel low, try reversing your hands. We also want to confirm which hand is which and to do this you will need a pendulum and/or a pair of clear quartz crystal points. The other reason for checking this is that the flow of energy through you seems to move in a particular direction and it is important not to block this by working in the opposite direction.

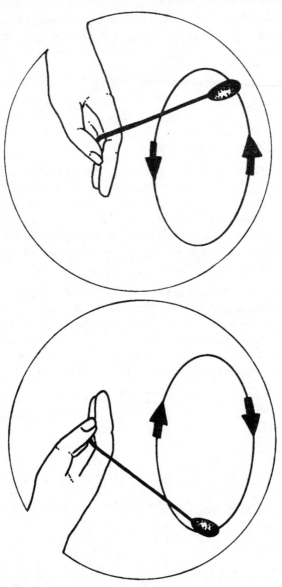

**Figure 11** Pendulum: yes and no

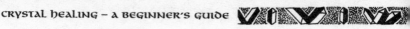

There are two ways of checking which is your receiving hand. The first is by using a pendulum and the second is a process of elimination. Using your pendulum should give you an accurate answer if you keep your head clear and do not allow any influencing thoughts to come into your mind. As the normal receiving hand is the left, take your pendulum in your right hand, and hold it over your open palm up left hand. Ask a very specific question 'is my left hand over which I am holding the pendulum my receiving hand?' The answer may take some time to come, so be patient. You should get either your yes or no symbol.

The second process requires a pair of quartz crystals as described in Chapter 3. First place one of the pair in the left hand with the point pointing up the arm; then place the other crystal in the right hand with the point pointing to the fingers. To tell if this is the right way for you leave the crystals in this position for a few minutes. If it feels uncomfortable or even painful put the crystals down before carrying on to the next part.

Next, reverse the direction of the crystals so that the one in the left hand is pointing towards the fingers and the crystal in the right hand is pointing up the arm. How does this feel when compared to the first direction? The way that feels most comfortable indicates the receiving hand is where the crystal is pointing up the arm and the sending hand where the crystal is pointing towards the fingers.

To eliminate one further aspect, change the crystals over in each hand and start again. It may be that the crystals are directional, in which case mark them as they are, the most comfortable way round, normally with the receiving crystal in the left hand. Use a dot of nail varnish or correcting fluid to mark one of the crystals and write down what the mark means. This is trial and error so you may have to go through this routine several times and as you obtain more crystals try it with these as well. Remember to be flexible about what happens.

# CONTRA INDICATIONS

This is an important aspect of all complementary therapies, when not to give a treatment. This may appear strange to start with but there is still a lot we do not understand, it is always better to be cautious. There are two sets of contra indications or when not to use crystals. The first relates to you: if you do not feel as if you want to use the crystals follow that feeling. If you do not want to work on a person, follow that feeling. If you feel that the situation may go beyond your capability, follow that feeling. If you are unwell or tired it is probably better not to use the crystals on other people, this may be a time to rest or when you need to work on yourself. Remember you have the right to say, 'No, I do not want to undertake this task'. You do not even have to give a reason.

The second set of contra indications relates to other people. At this stage do not to attempt to work on those with serious illnesses, women who are pregnant, those with heart problems, diabetes, epilepsy and asthma. In addition, if they are receiving regular treatment from a medical professional they may want to check with them first. If someone has cancer and are at the final stages of life then the attention can improve the quality of life but I suggest that for those who are undergoing treatment that you leave them alone. These decisions are up to you and the person who wants the treatment. One of the questions that has to be approached is why this particular person has this disease, and if they start to release the cause can you deal with that happening. Therefore, always ask about these types of problems before working on anyone and explain that you cannot work on them if they have any of them. Write down their responses. Look at the example question sheet in the appendix.

A commonly asked question with most types of therapy is when to stop. The answer, like a majority of this work, is an intuitive answer – when you think the time is right. If the situation is reaching a

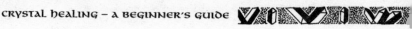

point where you feel that you cannot cope, carefully support the person and say that you have to bring the session to a close. You can then suggest that they seek further assistance and support. Give them time to deal with issues raised. This probably will not happen but if it does do not panic, stay grounded and you will cope.

Next follows a brief account of what can happen to those that you are working on, so you can be more prepared for their responses. When using crystals on an individual they may just lie there, they may shake, twitch or move suddenly, they may start to cry or even get angry. These are all normal reactions and the important thing is to remain calm and grounded, support them and reassure them as much as possible. In some situations, humour can help but not bawdy jokes! Remember that it is the individual who is actually undertaking the healing. We act only as a catalyst, so they may want to release whatever is happening to them. These type of responses do not happen every time, but it is important to be prepared for them, so always have a box of tissues handy.

Finally, at the end of the treatment time make sure that the person you have been working with is back amongst us and well grounded. Encourage them to get up slowly and not rush up. Give them a drink or a biscuit; ask them to name animals, flowers or family members. If they are still a bit floaty, a piece of hematite or a rock may help earth them or get them to touch the ground with their hands or stamp their feet. When you feel they are safe they can go but discourage them from driving immediately.

Explain to them that there may be some reaction to the treatment, called a *healing crisis*. It does not happen in all cases, when it does it can be mild or quite severe. It can be a runny nose or more visits to the toilet than normal; it can for a short while be an increase in the original symptoms of any complaint or a reoccurrence of an old, maybe forgotten problem. Again, explain that this is a normal and natural event caused by the body and mind realigning themselves to a change in circumstances and moving towards, hopefully, better health.

# PRACTICE

There are several exercises in this section to give you time to bring together the contents of this chapter.

First clear or clean the space you are going to use for your work. Physically clean the room and then smudge or burn essential oils. With smudging, you can walk around in a clockwise direction wafting the smudge smoke into all the corners. If you use essential oils, burn them in an essential oil diffuser with water, leave this for about an hour. As with all fire, do not leave the smudge or oil burner unattended. Make sure the smudge is properly extinguished as it can smoulder for a long time.

Now prepare yourself by going through the centring and grounding exercises, take your time over these to get the feel of them. Spend some time deciding what help you will use such as your guardian angel or power animal.

Next work through the feeling energy process, feel the energy between your hands. Try this several times over several days to see if you can pick up various layers.

Spend time with your clear quartz points. Feel the energy from the point, triangle and side. Note the difference between them. Repeat this exercise at least five times. Sit with each clear quartz crystal, centre and ground first, let your mind clear as much as possible and see if you can connect to the crystal. You can ask questions such as 'how can you help me?' or 'how can you help my work?' and see what answers you get. Note down all your results.

Work through the receiving and sending hand exercise to identify which hand is which. Write down your experiences.

# 5

# FINDING WHERE TO WORK

*This is where you are getting very close to actually working with your crystals on someone, the exciting part. Prepare the room and go through your centring and grounding exercise – the start up ritual. Call upon your deities or helpers.*

When they arrive welcome your guinea pig, take their coat, make them feel comfortable, ask them to sit down; it is nice if no one wears shoes, so ask them to leave their shoes at the door. Next, you need to obtain some information from this person and give them some as well. Normally you would go through a full history to build up a picture but as at this stage you will probably be working with someone you know well, all you have to be aware of are the contra indications as outlined in the previous chapter. Two good questions at this stage are 'Why do you want a treatment?', for which the answer will probably be 'Because you asked me' and the second is 'What do you expect from this session?'.

Ask them to lie down on what ever you are using, on their back, on cushions or bed. Ask them to relax as much as possible, to help with this ensure they are warm and comfortable. It is hard to relax when cold as the body is concentrating on surviving or when uncomfortable as that tends to be the main thing on the mind. If necessary, place small cushions under the small of the back and under the knees. These help reduce the stresses and strains on the body caused by lying flat on their back and, therefore, make the person more comfortable and able to relax.

# READINg THE pERSON

Now it is time to start feeling the person, their aura that is, not their body. You will do this several times in different ways during a treatment. Each time write down your findings; remember to trust your feelings, intuition and what you see or perceive. The first assessment is purely visual, look at the person, how do they seem, are there parts that look empty or full, flowing or congested? Write it down, an outline diagram of a person can help, and you can write little notes directly on the relevant parts. Next, look to the sides of them, look just above them and use your peripheral vision, the side of your eyes. What do you see? This peripheral visual scan may show areas where there is a hole or lack of energy, or you may not see anything just the person. Write down your findings.

If you have a pendulum prepare to use it. Working from the top of the head down the centreline of the body ask about the energy of each chakra, these are shown in Figure 12 and are discussed in the next section. By asking to see the energy level of the chakras you may get both clock and counter clockwise circles, horizontal movements and other types of swings. You will have to ascertain their true meaning. In general, a circle in either direction indicates energy is there and the chakra is active, the relative diameters of the circles indicate the amount of energy or strength of the chakra and its abilities. A horizontal backwards and forwards movement implies a blockage and a vertical swing can mean that the chakra has shut down or the energy is not being transformed by that chakra. There are very many versions of what the movements and meanings are for chakras, follow your intuition with what feels right for you. Again, note your findings.

The next method of obtaining information is to use your hands. You can use whichever hand you want, or even both hands. It is up to you, some people use their receiving hand, others find that for this type of work their sending hand is more powerful and receptive. You may find that it helps to rub your hands together before starting and at the end or during the feeling process to shake them off or flick

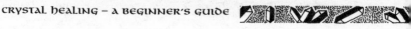

them to the earth. This releases any build up of energy and sends it for transmutation into positive energy by the earth. Remember that all of this work is for the common good of all.

Start at the top of the head, about 8 to 10 cm (3 or 4 inches) from the physical body and scan over the body. This means moving your hand backwards and forwards over the body and noting what you feel. This can be top to bottom over the body or from side to side. If you feel you need to move your hand up or down vertically do so and try to feel at what level you are working at, the physical, emotional, mental or spiritual. You may feel a balloon-like sensation, which indicates you are entering another auric layer.

As you work over the body you may pick up small changes, these may be hot or cold spots, fizzy feelings, twitches in your hand, feelings of draughts, or other very gentle and sometimes not so gentle feelings. At times you may feel that it is your imagination but believe in yourself and what you feel. The person on whom you are working may well give feedback as to what is happening to them. Some people find this a tickly experience; others can feel your hand working in their aura.

Note your findings, then sit quietly and let your intuition speak if it wants to. Again, note your findings. Then look at all of these findings together and see whether a picture is starting to come together. What can you say about this person, their energies and problems? What areas need work, which chakras are blocked or very energetic and may need calming down? What do you think needs to happen to them? Do they need slowing down or speeding up? Are they hiding something that your analysis has shown up? Do they seem to be loosing energy from a part of their body? Is there somewhere that seems empty or hollow? Are they putting their hands on their body in a protective manner, if so where and what do you think that means?

However, it is important to remember that you are not in a position to diagnoze about a person's health. That process requires a great deal of training and a great deal of practice. The Code of Conduct of most complementary therapy organizations forbids diagnosis for the client, only for decisions for the therapy.

Spend some time putting your picture together. When you have, select one or two places that seem to be the most important and make sure you have an idea of the energy levels of those places, even if it is a hunch or general feeling.

# Chakras

We now need to look at the chakras in more detail. Chakras, their positions, uses and properties have been recognized for thousands of years and on many continents. They are considered to be energy centres that exist inside, on and outside the body and to have many purposes and uses. They are very special places where external energy can enter the body and be redistributed. This external energy has also been recognized for thousands of years. It is referred to as ki, chi, prana, or universal energy. This energy is as important as food for the well being of the body, emotions and spirit. Each chakra is considered to deal with a different set of energies in the body, each one is also related to an endocrine gland and to a nerve plexus. This brings the orthodox and esoteric forms together.

They can also act as an indicator to show how energy is moving around the body and how shortages and excesses of particular energy within the body are affecting a person's health. The reason that chakras are of interest to crystal healing is that they can act both as a guide and as a place of energy absorption from crystals and then to other areas in the body. As we work through the body, it is often the chakra points that provide an indication as to the health of an individual. The chakras can be identified and assessed with a pendulum and by using the scanning process of the hand.

As a guide use Figure 12. You can move over the chakra points and begin to feel where they are. Each one is likely to be different and each one on each person is likely to be different. Although they have different energies, it is possible to find them by scanning and asking where they are, but sometimes you may not feel some or all of them. This is achieved by going to the approximate place and moving your hand around. There will also be a difference in feeling caused by the

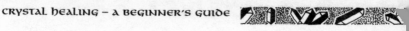

way that you interact with each person. Chakras are important to your work as they can be used as a starting point for the healing process.

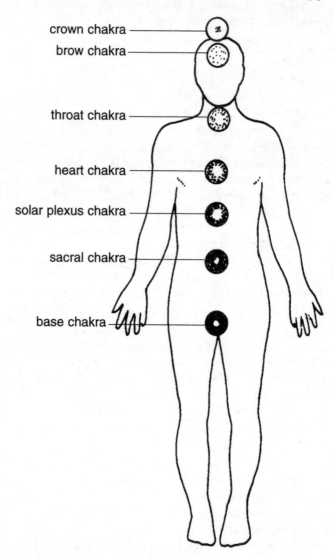

crown chakra
brow chakra
throat chakra
heart chakra
solar plexus chakra
sacral chakra
base chakra

**Figure 12** Chakras

As you feel over people, you may become aware of other feelings of energy. These may be static with cool or hot spots or flowing and may move up or down the body. There is a lot of movement of energy in and around the body with many interpretations. In general, energy can be considered to flow up the back of the body and down the front or from top to bottom. The important aspect of this is that the energy is flowing. If you do not feel any of this do not worry, it can take time for the mind to accept information that it is not used to handling. Sometimes when feeling over the body a particular feeling may occur over a large part of the body such as a leg or arm. What you may be feeling is the meridian energy flow, one of the energy channels that circulate throughout the body. These are used in chinese medicine, acupuncture, acupressure, shiatsu and in crystal healing.

Finally, when someone has indicated that a particular area is painful scan it carefully allowing yourself to feel the energy or lack of from that area. Occasionally you may even pick up the same pain in your own body. If this happens let the pain go and increase your own protective layer by visualizing yourself in a cocoon of violet or golden light.

This process should have given you an insight into the areas that need to be worked upon. It is not possible to be precise as to what feeling indicates what, as this varies from worker to worker and person to person. However, as a guide here are some of the feelings that may occur: you may feel a sticky, gunky layer all over someone, this is sometimes a build up of negative energy absorbed by that person, or from the use of alcohol or drugs. Hot or cold patches may be over or under use, particularly of a chakra; an empty feeling may be just that, an empty chakra point that needs re-energizing; tingly feeling may indicate movement of energy that needs calming; burning sensation may be an overactive area. Each time you feel a sensation try to relate it to what is happening to the individual. Record your observations as soon as possible so that you can look back at them after a healing session to see what has happened.

# Auras

Having looked briefly at the chakras it is also important to consider the auras that surround the body. Auras are the different layers that are said to surround the body. They are visible to those who have the ability to see them and it is possible for some people to learn how to see them. If you cannot see them do not worry, most people cannot, however, you have probably already felt them. There are many views as to the number of auric layers, what they represent and what they are like. Again, you have to find an interpretation that suits your own feelings. Auras are supposed to surround all living things, from animals to plants. Auras have also been photographed using Kirlian Photography and used in health diagnosis.

The first few layers seem to have an agreed layout. The first layer which can be between 1 to 10 or 12 cm (0.25 of an inch to 4 or 5 inches) above the body is the physical layer, this is supposed to be the plan for the body, either to grow into or to hold information that tells it how to grow. The second layer is the emotional layer and deals with the emotional aspect of our lives providing information about emotional issues. The third layer is the mental layer, all physical things are supposed to start with a thought. Without the idea, there is no product. Beyond the mental layer, there is a level of uncertainty. These spiritual layers relate to the interconnectedness of all things.

The auras seem to work in many ways, consider how we relate to different people and different situations. If you are in a crowded room there are two things that can happen that relate to the aura, first you feel uncomfortable as people get to close. They are entering your auric layers without permission. If someone you know well enters the room behind you, you may sense them before you turn around. Your two sets of auras know each other's patterns, are acceptable and maybe even communicate with each other. These two apparently opposite situations are two different aspects of the same function.

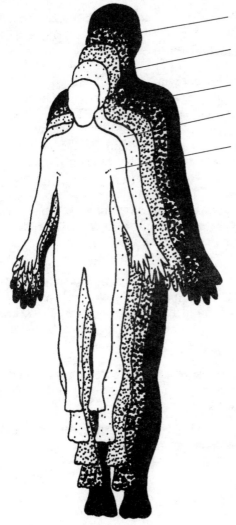

**Figure 13** Auras

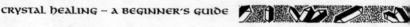
# PRACTICE

The first two exercises involve the chakras and auras. The first is to find as many of your own chakras and auric layers as possible. Centre and ground yourself and then with your preferred hand feel a little way out from your body over the areas where the chakras exist. Gently move your hand around until you feel something. It may be a very small feeling of heat, cold or tingling. Remember that place, or you can mark it with a suitable marker pen, and move on to the next one. If you are not noticing anything, try moving your hand in and out with respect to your body. Another way to find your chakras is to find small indentations on the body. This seems to work for many of them. The throat chakra is in the hollow just above the top of the sternum. The heart chakra is on the sternum and there is a slight indentation about 3 cm (1½ inches) from the bottom of the sternum. Try finding the rest of them. The base chakra indentation is between the anus and the genitals.

Now for the auras, try feeling your own auric layers and see how many you can find. Use your palm and work from the outside in. Slowly bring your hand parallel to your body, in small backward and forwards movements. It is important to keep your hand relaxed as you do this.

The second part is to try working with a partner to find their chakras and auras. Return to the relevant section in this chapter and follow the directions.

Take your time with these exercises. If possible, repeat them several times to assist in the growth of your abilities.

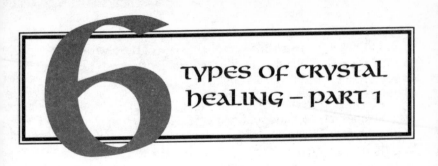

## BASIC INSTRUCTIONS

You have obtained your information from and about your client and now comes the time to start using the crystals. The client was asked to lie down at the beginning of the previous chapter, which is why you should read the book before starting work on people. Please remember that you are working at a very subtle level and need to move yourself and your crystals carefully and gently when near to this person. Keep the crystals you are about to use, and those you have already used, well away from each other and the person lying down. This is because you do not want the influence of the new crystals to necessarily be in the area and you do not want them reabsorbing any negative energy from the used stones.

You may want to tell them how long the session will take; this first part should take about 10 minutes, and the second stage of laying crystals on about 20 minutes. These times will vary depending on what work you carry out.

If the client wants to talk let them do so. Try to keep the talk concerned with what is going on for them rather than the weather or what their nextdoor neighbour was saying. Where possible say as little as possible, do not get caught up in the conversation. Remember that an important part of the treatment is in the idea that this is a place of relaxation.

Make sure that the person lying down is still comfortable and suggest, if they have not done so, that they close their eyes and

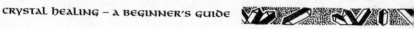
continue to relax as much as possible. The process of relaxing is a great aid to self-healing; this is probably one of the few times in most of their adult life that they have actually stopped. If you feel it is appropriate, you could lead them through a little relaxing meditation.

As relaxation of the mind and body are related try a physical relaxation first. The idea is to forcibly tighten or tense their muscles and then relax them, as they relax them, they can feel the wonderful difference. Before trying this on other people run through it yourself. As they lie there ask them to clench the muscles in their feet, starting with the toes and working upwards to below the ankles. After about 5 seconds, tell them to release, relax and to notice the difference. Slowly work up through the body, tensing and relaxing as follows: toes, feet, ankles, calves, knees, thighs, perineum, buttocks, lower abdomen front and back, mid abdomen front and back, chest area front and back, shoulders, upper arm, lower arm, hands, neck, face, mouth, tongue, nose, eyes, forehead and, finally, the whole body and then a full relax.

The client is now in a quiet relaxed state so it is time to start work.

# Using single terminated quartz crystals

The first action may be to clear away the layer of gunk around the person. This can be done as a routine start to the treatment, as it is a clearing and relaxing activity. Take one of your clear quartz crystal points and hold it between thumb and forefinger so that the crystal is nearly at right angles to your arm. The part of the crystal to use is the blade, the side. With gentle sweeping movements sweep down from the middle of the body to the ground with the intent that any negative energy is removed and grounded. You can start at about the level of the heart chakra and work all over the body in a

clockwise direction. When you get to the top of the legs work down the first leg several times and then move round to the second leg. Work between 5 and 10 cm (2 and 4 inches) above the body. When you have worked all the way round and returned to the starting point sweep from the head down to the feet several times covering all of the body. Now shake your crystal asking that any negative energy be transmuted for the good of all. When you get more crystals including a wand, a shaped crystal, use that for this exercise. A rose quartz wand can provide a supportive caring feeling as the gunk is cleared away.

Refer back to your information from the client, both what they said and from your pendulum and scanning analysis. If there were any areas that felt blocked or where there was pain, now is the time to work on them.

This process is in two stages, the first is the removal of negative energy, and the second is replacing the negative energy with positive energy, removal and infusion. You will need a single clear quartz crystal. Place your crystal in your sending hand with the point facing away from the hand; place this hand down by your side away from your client. Now put your receiving hand just above the area that you feel requires clearing, visualize the negative energy being pulled out and passing through you to the crystal. Remember to stay relaxed, if you tense up your ability to feel energy will decrease.

Now turn the crystal in a counter-clockwise direction seeing the negative energy going into the ground to be dealt with safely. Remember that the energy should pass straight through you; do not let it become part of you. As you clear the area the feeling in your sending hand may change, becoming harder to turn or the sensation in you receiving hand may alter in some subtle way. You must at this stage trust your judgement, but a few minutes of clearing should be enough at this stage.

It is important to replace the negative energy you have now removed with positive energy, rather than leaving a void. To do this you reverse the process. Keep the crystal in your sending hand; shake it

**Figure 14** Circling anti-clockwise

to ground to clear it, or blow on it with the intent of clearing away any retained negative energy, and place it over the area you are working on. Shake your other hand to clear it and place it so that it is to the side of the client and the palm is facing upwards. Relax and visualize healing energy being received by your receiving hand and passing through to your sending hand and the crystal, as you do so

move your sending hand in a clockwise circle over the area of concern. Keep doing this until you feel there has been a sufficient influx of positive energy. Again this may be a change of sensation in your receiving hand or that the sending hand gets harder to turn as if you have filled the empty space. Ask the client how they feel, they may have no sensation at all, any pain may be gone, the area may feel warm or some other response.

Congratulations you have accomplished your first crystal healing.

**Figure 15**  Circling clockwise

# USING TWO CLEAR QUARTZ CRYSTALS

The previous healing used your hand as part of the process, in fact, if necessary, the receiving hand can be placed on the body. The next exercise uses two clear quartz points, one in each hand. This is does not mean that it is twice as effective, rather, it moves the energy in a different way. In some respects, it could be said to be more precise. The process is basically the same, this time with a crystal in each hand; one in your sending hand and the other in your receiving hand.

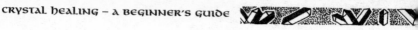

Decide on the area that needs clearing. In your receiving hand, hold the clear quartz terminated crystal in your fingers; point towards your wrist, so that the blunt end is just sticking out past the end of your fingers. In the sending hand, place the clear quartz crystal with the pointed end sticking out. Hold your receiving hand with its crystal over the area to be cleared and your sending crystal pointing down, as before, away from the body. To draw out negative energy relax and visualize the energy going into the receiving crystal and through your arms to your sending crystal which you are turning in a counter-clockwise direction. Continue until you feel that you have removed as much negative energy as possible.

Now you need to infuse the area with positive energy, this is similar to the single crystal process. You can clear your pair of crystals with a shake to the earth or by blowing on them. Place your sending hand over the body with the crystal pointing down and your receiving hand palm up with the crystal pointing towards your wrist. Relax and visualize healing energy coming into your receiving hand and passing through the crystal to your sending hand and crystal. Rotate the sending hand in a clockwise direction over the area you have been working on. After a while this will begin to feel full and it is time to stop. Check with your client that they are feeling OK and find out what reaction they had, if any. You have now completed your second method of working with crystals.

These two methods can be used for a variety of healing situations. They can be used for both over active and under active energy levels. If the area is under active or empty, the clearing process may be very quick. Keep alert for changes in your hands, as you do not want to deplete the area any more than necessary but you do want to clear away any negativity. Although this has been said many times – learn to trust your own intuition. If in doubt stop, don't carry on regardless, ground yourself, relax and reassess the situation. At any stage of these treatments you can stop and feel the energy above the area you are working on and reassess the situation. You can also ask the client how they feel, whether they are noticing any new sensations in their body or mind.

**Figure 16** Energy in and out (hands)

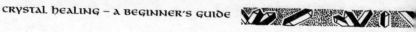

At the end of either of these two processes you can sweep over the body with the blade of the clear quartz to clear away any negativity that may be in the aura, it can also act like a gentle massage in a calming and soothing manner. Remember to ask the negative energy to be taken to the ground.

The important thing is to practise these techniques before going on to the next stage. Although there seems to be more preparation than action, the preparation is part of the healing process. The important thing to remember is the trusting of your own intuition and the responses that you notice.

# Room cleansing

After giving any healing treatment the room in which you have been working is likely to contain some of the removed negative energy. It is important to clear this out of the way. Several methods can be used quickly and effectively. The first is to open as many windows as possible to let the air circulate. Next, a good smudging session can have a dramatic effect especially with open windows. Lighting a candle or burning juniper oil in an essential oil vaporizer also helps. Try not to use the room while it is clearing and be conscious of not absorbing any of this negative energy.

## PRACTICE

These exercises are the real thing. This is where you practise what you learnt in this chapter. Here is a checklist of events.

1 Prepare workroom.
2 Prepare yourself.
3 Centre, ground and request helpers.
4 Make helper comfortable.
5 Ask about health and why they have come to you.
6 Make them comfortable lying down.
7 Check your grounding and helpers.
8 Use your pendulum and note results.
9 Use your hand to scan and note results.
10 Select one or two places to work, if the other person has a specific area work on that.
11 Use one crystal to remove and replace.
12 Use two crystals to remove and replace.
13 Check that the other person is grounded and safe to leave.
14 Clean your crystals as necessary.
15 Cleanse your room.
16 Write up your notes as a record.

# TYPES OF CRYSTAL HEALING – PART 2

*This section looks at using crystals placed on the body, perhaps in a way that you have imagined crystal healing to be like. For this section you will need most of the stones discussed earlier and Figure 12, the chakras.*

## What the crystal feels like

Before you place a single stone on an individual, it is important that you have experienced what effect the stone is likely to have. This is because we are using fine levels of energy and the experience will assist you in making a decision as to whether you should use those particular stones. The first set of crystals we will look at have been used by a large number of people and in general there is an accepted use for them. Get to know your stones first, this may seem a long process but there are only eight in this basic set and a few quiet sessions will start to give you an idea of their powers. This process is also part of developing your own attunement and abilities that will be needed when using crystals in a more intuitive manner.

Start by returning to your centring and grounding exercise, which by now will be taking less time and will probably be feeling stronger, possibly giving you more confidence when working with these types of energy. Sit quietly for a few moments and then pick up the stone you wish to work with, having previously placed it nearby. Hold the crystal between the palms of your two hands and make sure they remain comfortable. Your hands can be on your lap or held in front of you in the classic prayer position. These seem to be good

positions giving the stone and your energy field a strong interaction. You may wish to try other ways of holding the stone including in either hand, flat or fist like, with the other hand possibly placed under the holding hand. You can place the crystal on the relevant part of your body, such as on the chakra for which the stone is intended, but do as you feel, not what the book says; or on another part of your body where the stone seems drawn towards.

Simply sit with the stone; you can focus on the stone or let your mind stay as blank as possible. If other thoughts about daily issues come into focus let them go, try encapsulating them into a balloon and allowing them to drift away. After sitting quietly with your stone for a while you may start to notice one or more of the following types of reaction:

1 Part of your body may start to feel different; the energy of the crystal may be working in an area that is in need of that particular energy. Note the changes taking place, at the same time staying in that calm relaxed state.

2 There may be unpleasant feelings in your arms; this normally is a reaction to the crystal. Try changing hands or holding the crystal in one hand or if it is too disagreeable put the stone down. It may be that the stone is not right for you now, however with the first set of stones this form of reaction is unlikely. If there is, put the stone down immediately, shake your hands, pick up a piece of rose quartz and hold that for a while.

3 There may be a change in your thoughts; you may start to feel calmer, energized, peaceful, forgiving or fidgety. You may have glimpses of vivid pictures in your mind, these may have no meaning to you or they may start to explain other feelings you have had. The crystals can often help you in putting together a fuller picture of who and what you are. If this process becomes unpleasant then put the stone down, take several good deep breaths, pick up a rose quartz and a hematite stone and hold them for a while. You may want to return to your original stone and try again.

4 The crystal in some other way may affect you. For example, you may see colours or a wash of colour going through your mind. You may pick up feelings that were not with you before. You may

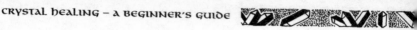

see visions of all sorts of things or even obtain information about the way that the crystal can assist you either directly or in your work.

5 You may not feel or see anything at all. Do not worry as no one can work with the crystals all the time. There may be several reasons why this has happened. You may be tired, a common problem in these busy days, just try again when you are feeling more refreshed. A 20-minute meditation, or a catnap, may be enough to help, after which you can try again. If you have been working on your crystals at night and found it hard, try to do these exercises in the morning when you feel refreshed. It is important at all times not to try too hard, as this will also reduce your innate abilities. You may be having one of those days where it just won't happen or you may be over concerned by other activities and your mind cannot calm down enough. If you are having a day where your emotions have been strained then your heart may be too busy, so look after yourself and try again later.

6 As stated before you may get an urge to place the stone on your body. If this happens just follow that urge and hold the stone where it feels right. Try to remember the sensations and the reactions that occur.

7 Finally, you may have an impulse to ask the crystal all sorts of questions. You can also try this if you do not have any response to the stone with other methods. You can ask what the stone can do, what its purpose is, how it can help you and your work and any thing else that seems pertinent. You can also ask to see the *diva*. This is the spirit of the stone and of all stones of a similar kind. How the diva will appear varies from person to person but it seems that the basic concept remains the same. For a particular stone one person may get a soft image, another a pale or pink colour and a third fluffy clouds but they all have a common factor in the image of softness. There may also be differences between stones of the same type and different occasions with the same stone. Any questions can be asked in silence or aloud depending on your situation.

Always take a break between stones, as you do not want the influence of the previous stone on the new response. Make sure you

ground and re-centre each time. Get up and move around; shake your hands and arms, clear your mind ready to start again. If you feel light headed or a little bit out of it try sniffing some patchouli oil, eating a snack, holding a hematite stone or a rock to help bring your self down to earth.

# The STONES

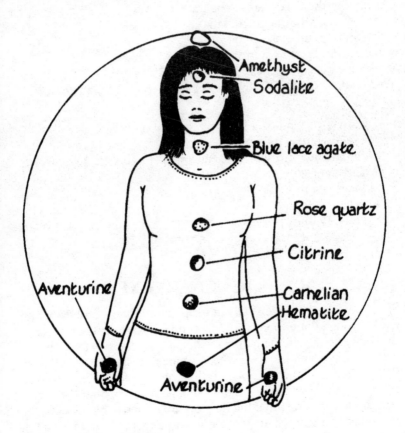

**Figure 17** Chakra layout

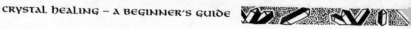

There are many types of stones that can be used on each chakra; this is not the place to provide many different lists, as they would probably cause confusion. It is better at this stage to concentrate on a few and then work with others as the time and space arises. The first basic chakra set consists of:

- amethyst for the crown chakra
- sodalite for the brow chakra
- blue lace agate for the throat chakra
- rose quartz for the heart chakra
- citrine for the solar plexus chakra
- carnelian for the sacral chakra
- hematite for the base chakra
- aventurine to be held in the hands for balance.

As well as their properties, these stones virtually follow the chakra colour pattern with the rainbow approach to the chakra colours.

- amethyst is violet
- sodalite is dark blue
- blue lace agate is pale blue
- rose quartz is pink, which some consider to be the heart colour rather than green
- citrine is yellow
- carnelian is orange
- hematite is shiny on the outside but when rubbed on a porcelain tile, used for testing crystals, it streaks red.

# FEELING THE CRYSTALS

Sit with each of these crystals in turn, start with the amethyst and work through them. If you do this in one session look for the differences between them as you change stones as well as the feeling from each one. Give yourself time to respond to each stone. By working from the top down to the bottom you should slowly become more grounded as the session goes on. If, after two stones, you are not picking anything up stop, try a lower chakra stone, such as hematite or carnelian, and see what happens. If there is still no reaction do not worry, stop and try again at another time. Use the time you have allotted to this exercise to meditate or rest.

After each stone, write down your findings. This is important, as it is easy for the new information to wipe out the old material and the whole session to become a confused memory.

If you work with each stone at different times, you may want to use the hematite after each session, again to help return you to this plain. This is particularly important after sitting with the three top chakra stones, amethyst, sodalite and blue lace agate, whose energies are of a reasonably high level. You may also find that you are energetic after holding some of the stones, this is part of their function to increase energy levels.

As well as sitting with the stones you can spend longer with them, keep them close to you on a daily basis and also keep a notebook with you to record any reactions, events or thoughts. Try this for each stone for three days or more. This may give you a deeper insight into the power and energies of each crystal.

# Chakra Layout 1

Having worked through the eight stones it is now time to try them on yourself all at once. Do not do this in the same session as the individual learning sessions. This is a basic chakra balance and will give you an idea what the chakra balance feels like, it is not quite the same as having someone there but the effect will help you appreciate what may happen to other people. This is not the easiest task but with a little bit of care, it can be achieved. Remember that it is important to relax when the crystals are on you, so ensure that you will feel comfortable having placed the stones on yourself. For this exercise, you will need to place the hematite just below your feet and the amethyst just above your head. Then you can lie down and place then the carnelian on the sacral chakra just below the navel; the citrine on the solar plexus which is just below the breast bone; the rose quartz on the heart chakra which is between the breasts. The blue lace agate goes in the indentation at the throat and the sodalite on the forehead just above the eyebrows. These

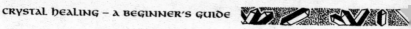

should all be in a straight line along the centre of the body but unless you have a mirrored ceiling, you will not be able to confirm this. Place a piece of aventurine in each hand and gently hold it. Try to relax with the crystals on you, don't tense up trying to stop them falling or moving.

As you relax let any feelings wash over you. Do not try to feel what is happening, just note anything that happens or any feelings or sensations that come into your mind. If a stone should fall off just let it be, it may mean that it should not be there or that its work is complete. After about 20 minutes take the crystals off, start at the top and work down. Sit up slowly and check how you feel. Write down your results even if they are, 'I didn't feel anything'.

Now, you have a basic knowledge of how the crystals may feel and what they may do for other people. With this, you can now use them on a friend to see how they can assist them.

# Chakra Layout 2

For this, you require someone else's body. You need to start at the beginning and go through all the preparation and start-up routines. When the person you are working on arrives make them comfortable and at ease. This does not have to be done in a sombre and serious mode; on the other hand, it is not a flippant activity. It is a good idea to have them remove their shoes when they enter the treatment space. Go through the questions about health and ask them to lie down. Again, make sure they will be comfortable. Place a cushion under the small of the back and knees. Also have a blanket available to cover them if they get cold in the middle of the session; this can be placed over the crystals once they are in place or the crystals can be placed on the blanket. It is not uncommon for people to feel cool during crystal healing sessions, this is because they have relaxed and are keeping relatively still.

Go through the pendulum and scanning procedures to feel the energy states before the treatment. Then start placing the crystals on the person. Remember this is a balancing layout rather than a healing session.

The first crystal to place is the hematite. This is placed at the base chakra. It is often difficult to get this stone in place because of the shape of the body (both male and female) and the nature of the clothing. The best thing to do is place it just above the lower extremities of the body, or even slightly higher depending on the clothing. Next, place the amethyst at the top of the head. If this is a terminated stone point the termination towards the head. Then place the other stones on the body from the sacral upwards. Finally, place a piece of aventurine in each of their hands. Move away from them and keep quiet. If they want to chatter suggest that they close their eyes and relax, to think about somewhere nice like a beach or the woods. If they want to talk about what is happening to them that is fine. Just listen and respond with interest and empathy, but do not start making suggestions as to how they can change their lives.

After 20 minutes scan over them again to see if there are any changes. Normally there will be. Afterwards, if they ask, you can explain what you did and what you found but remember that this is not a medical diagnosis or treatment. Be careful not to diagnoze any illnesses and frighten people. Just because the energy level was low does not mean it is cancer, rather that they may have had a busy time. Let them relax for a few minutes whilst their own system adjusts to the energy changes. Help them up slowly, do not leave them on their own until you are sure that they are well grounded, give them another piece of hematite to hold for a while or a sniff of patchouli if necessary. Get any feedback you can from them and write that down as soon as possible.

That is it, your first chakra balance complete. The more you do, the more you will be able to do. Sometimes the energy will be fine and you may not want to put a crystal on that chakra. At other times, you may want to combine the action of the clear quartz with the chakra stones; these are methods discussed later in this chapter.

When you have taken the stones off make sure they are kept well away from the person you have been working on and are cleaned as needed. Remember that they may contain negative energy from the client, which is why they should not handle them afterwards in case they reabsorb the energy that has been removed.

# The next stage

The chakra balance is a very gentle way of working with crystals; it helps the body look at itself and to start relaxing and bring itself on the path towards balance. The next stage is to start the same process more effectively using the same set of crystals. The stage after that would be to use different crystals, that is beyond the range of this book. This part will use the same crystals as before but it utilizes more of the information gained from the person, pendulum and scans.

In the previous example, before you placed the crystals on the person, you felt over them with your hands and pendulum. You also looked at them. What did you pick up, what did you see? Use this type of information together with your knowledge of the eight stones used in the chakra layout to make decisions as to which stone should be placed where. It is important to have worked with the chakra layout several times before attempting this process to see the relationship and changes between crystals, energies and chakras.

With each treatment start from the beginning with your start up routines. Find out about the client, their medical history, how they feel now and what they expect from this session. At this stage it may be of help to remember the relationships between the chakras and the glands of the body, the table below gives the outline of this, there are, however, several versions.

| Crown | Pituitary |
|-------|-----------|
| Brow | Pineal |
| Throat | Thyroid |
| Heart | Heart |
| Solar plexus | Pancreas |
| Sacral | Gonads |
| Base | Adrenals |

So how do you put all this together? Start with getting all the information, look, scan and use the pendulum. Some parts will seem to be more energetic, warmer, stronger, slower, weaker or just different. This difference may be a stodgy, gluey feeling, an electric feeling, sharp pains, or sudden changes in temperature. Write down your results.

Place the standard chakra layout on the person and again feel over them remembering what you had felt earlier. Now, using your clear quartz point, work on those areas that seemed different. If they were sluggish or gluey, try scraping away the gunk with the blade of the

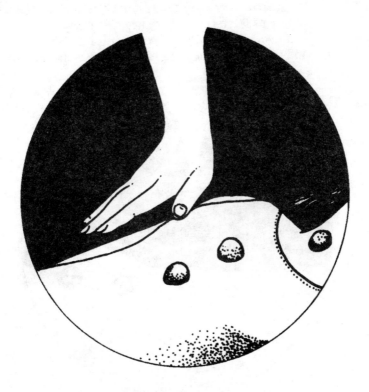

**Figure 18** Feeling over chakra stone

quartz, as you move this energy away from the person ensure that you visualize it going into the ground to be transmuted for the good of all. If there is stodginess all over them clear away all over them, if it is in a band, either vertically or horizontally work from both sides bringing the energy to the earth. Remember not to intrude into the individual's space to much as you work on them, so move around them rather than leaning across. The more you intrude the greater the interaction between your energy and that of the person you are working on. This type of clearing is often needed on those who have a lot of contact with other people. An example would be someone who works in a shop, as customers bring all their negative energy with them. The act of shopping in towns and cities can be stressful. As the assistant helps them some of the negative energy is transferred from the customer. Over a period this builds up into a sticky mess and may be detrimental to their energetic health.

**Figure 19** Cleaning gunk with blade

Having cleared the overall gunk layers out of the way, you can concentrate on specific areas. Start with an area over and around a chakra. Feel over the area again and if you feel that it is appropriate use the spiralling technique with either one or two clear quartz points. Remove the layout crystal and put it to one side.

To remove the negative energy place a clear quartz point in both hands, in the receiving hand have the point pointing up the arm and in the sending hand have the point pointing out and away. Hold the receiving hand over the area to be worked on and hold the sending hand away from the person pointing down to the ground. Circle the sending hand in the anti-clockwise direction to pull out the negative energy.

When it feels right, stop, and replace the layout crystal. Shake the quartz points to earth or blow on them to remove any retained negative energy. Place your sending hand and crystal over the layout crystal. Hold out your receiving hand and clockwise circle the sending hand towards the layout crystal. The clear quartz crystal then passes its energy through the layout crystal increasing its effectiveness. This gives an added boost to that part of the body and aura of the area concerned.

This method can be repeated on several of the chakra stones. To start with, it would be a good idea to limit this to two areas. It can be a powerful process. By limiting the number of actions, you give the person a chance to assimilate the changes. Because there is a connection between all the parts of the body, you need to be aware of any changes that take place. It is possible that by changing one the person will automatically adjust the others.

This type of work gives you more flexibility as to where and for how long you work. There are no time limits on how much you should use the clear quartz points but just a few minutes should be more than enough. At this time in your work, stop sooner than later. The whole treatment should not take longer than 30 minutes from beginning to end.

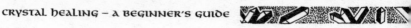

# The second advanced method

Having enhanced the power of the crystals using clear quartz it is now time to consider using fewer crystals. When you check the person with your hands and pendulum, some of the chakras may feel just right, not too active and not too sluggish. Although placing a crystal on them will do no harm, you may feel that you really want to concentrate on one or two of the other chakras. If this is so then you need to know which stones to use. Even just having seven basic crystals, of which you now have a good knowledge, you have a strong armoury with which to work. So start with a new person, otherwise the original one will have been lying there for several hours or even days! Go through your normal starting procedures and when the person is lying down scan over them in the normal way; if, and only if, you feel that some of their chakras are fine, think about what the other chakras may need. To do this just sit quietly for a few moments and see what comes into your mind, you may get a picture, a colour, or a feeling of a particular type of energy. If nothing comes into your mind just breathe gently and let yourself relax further into a kind of meditative state and again see what happens, remember not to fall asleep.

To start with, you may want to clear away a sticky layer. Do this, repeat your scanning to see if this has changed any of the chakras, and review what you feel you should do. As a guide, you know which crystals energize and which can calm things down and can apply that knowledge. If you have been picking up hot and cold sensations you may wish to consider the effect of the different colours of the stones and how these can be applied. It may be that you feel that you want to use your clear quartz first and then reassess the situation before applying a layout stone.

As you have been thinking about which crystals to place where, have any ideas come to you about what crystals are required for a particular chakra? If they have, then carry on with the treatment; if not try holding each crystal in turn and asking it some questions, silently in this case. Ask whether it can help this chakra, or whether this is a good one for this purpose. Listen carefully for any answers.

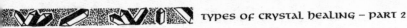 

If none come, use your pendulum. This method has been deliberately been left to last to give you time to start developing your intuitive processes. With the pendulum over each stone in turn, ask whether you should use this one on this particular chakra. As with all of these process concentrate only on one chakra at a time. When you have the stone for that chakra carry on to the next, clearing your mind first. For the first attempt, working on one chakra should be enough. It can also require more stones than you may have at present, so as your collection grows so can your choice.

An important factor that must be remembered all of the time is that the person lying there has put themselves in your hands and you have to watch over and monitor them. Do not go off and answer the telephone or make a cup of tea. Monitor them for change; in the way they breathe, tears running down from their eyes, shakes or twitches. All these things give you clues and feedback as to what is happening. These are all signs of release and generally mean that a perfectly normal reaction is taking place. Your job is to quietly support the person. In this situation try to be empathetic and supportive. Do not recount stories of what happened to you or give strong advice. Do not try to cheer them up until they have finished their release, however there is no need to be sombre about it either.

If a person comes to you with a specific problem try to relate that to the chakras and the stones. This is advanced work and beyond the scope of this book. However, do remember that if someone is not sleeping well it may not be a good idea to cover him or her in energetic stones and, if someone is lethargic, go carefully with the calming stones. Crystal healing is only a catalyst; the symptoms are a guide that there is something wrong or out of balance energetically. These forms of healing are holistic and it is not enough to remove the symptoms. Over a period, it is of far greater help to guide the individual to the root cause of the symptom. Then assist them in clearing that out of the way, thus removing the cause of the symptom.

You can also understand why continued treatments can act in a preventive manner by helping to keep the body in balance. This helps stop the build up of problems that can then lead to illness.

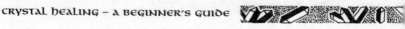

# PRACTICE

This set of exercises again utilizes the methods outlined in the chapter. The three methods in this chapter are:

- chakra layout
- chakra layouts with clear quartz assistance
- placing crystals using information from scans and pendulum.

Although they are all different the following checklist will give you a guide. If necessary, you can work back through the chapter.

1 Prepare your workspace.
2 Prepare yourself.
3 Obtain information from the person you are going to work on.
4 Get them comfortable.
5 Use your eyes, pendulum and scan.
6 Note your results.
7 For chakra balance, place the relevant crystals on them, starting at the bottom, let them enjoy the space for 20 minutes and remove the crystals starting at the top.
8 For chakra balance plus clear quartz work, place the crystals on them starting from the bottom, from your information select one or two chakras to work on and use the clear quartz points to remove and replace energy. Remember to use your intuition and to ground any negative energy. After 20 minutes, remove the stones from the top down.
9 For the advanced chakra balance decide on which chakra needs which type of energy and select the relevant stones. Place these on the person, check that they feel all right and leave for no longer than 20 minutes. Check with your hand or pendulum every 5 minutes and remove if you feel it is time.

In all three cases check that the person feels safe and grounded at the end. If necessary, help them to ground. Also, obtain as much feedback as possible.

Repeat these exercises several times, on different people.

# WHAT NEXT?

*If you have read the book, gone back and done all the practical exercises, you will have reached the stage of working with crystals on friends and family. The next stage is to keep practising. This can be broken into two parts. The first is stay in contact with your crystals. When you get a chance sit with them and listen to them. Also, try keeping the stone with you for several days and see what effect this has. Keep a journal of all your results so that you can go back and refresh your memory when needed.*

At this stage, you may find yourself increasing the size of your crystal collection, both with more of existing stones and with new stones you have not worked with before. In both these cases remember how to choose, cleanse and energize the crystals. It is also useful to spend time with the new crystals even if you have some of that type already.

You may find it useful to enrol on a crystal healing course, there are a few about, some run by local adult education centres and others privately by crystal healers or crystal schools. After that, you may want to consider training to become a crystal healer. There are several schools around and the qualification, a diploma, usually takes about two years to complete.

Keep adding to your knowledge and keep practising belief in your intuition.

In the meanwhile there are many books on the subject as well as associated subjects such as colour, chakras, subtle energy and vibrational medicine. These are listed in Further Reading at the end

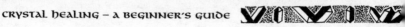

of this book. Some may be available from your local library and from specialist bookshops.

Also, several books in this series are useful background reading, such as:

*Gems and Crystals* by Kristyna Arcarti, 1994
*Working With Colour* by Pauline Willis, 1997
*Spiritual Healing* by Kristyna Arcarti, 1996
*Shamanism* by Teresa Moorey, 1997
*Reiki* by Sandi Leir Shuffrey, 1998
*Chakras* by Naomi Ozaniec, 1994

# appendix

## Sample question form

| INFORMATION REQUIRED | REASON FOR NEEDING INFORMATION |
|---|---|
| Name | As a record. |
| Address | In case you need to contact them. |
| Date | So you know when you saw them. |
| Date of birth | Helps with the overall picture. |
| Telephone number | In case you have to cancel. |
| Medical and surgical history | To help build up a picture and to start checking for contra indications. |
| Do they suffer from: heart condition, asthma, epilepsy, severe mental problem; are you pregnant? | Do not work with them. |
| Reason for visit | Gives further information. |
| Other information | |
| Findings from: | So you can learn from what you found. |

Looking
Scan
Pendulum

Record of treatment, where worked, timings, reactions

To provide you with a history and a means of seeing what working for this person.

(Use a separate sheet for subsequent sessions.)

You don't need to ask all the same questions again.

How did you feel after last time?

An important indicator.

Record of treatment, where worked, timings, reactions.

This is a brief outline for keeping records, to help you remember what happened and what you did. If the person comes back again then use a short form to record how they felt and any reactions they had.

# FURTHER READING

There have been many people and books that have provided the core of information from which the ideas in this book were drawn, this list gives a basic set of books for further reading on the subjects mentioned.

(All dates relate to editions to hand)

Baer & Baer, *Windows of Light*, Harper San Francisco, 1984 and *The Crystal Connection*, Harper San Francisco, 1987

Itzhak Bentov, *Stalking the Wild Pendulum*, Destiny, 1988

Barbara Ann Brennan, *Hands of Light*, Bantam, and *Light Emerging*, Bantam, 1993

Chase and Pawlik, *The Newcastle Guide to Healing with Crystals*, Newcastle, 1988 and *The Newcastle Guide to Healing with Gemstones*, Newcastle, 1989

John Davidson, *Subtle Energy*, C W Daniel, 1993

Thorwald Dethlefsen, *The Healing Power of Illness*, Element

Joy Gardener, *Color and Crystals*, The Crossing Press, 1988

Richard Gerber, *Vibrational Medicine*, Bear & Co, 1988

Michael Harner, *The Way of the Shaman*, Harper San Francisco, 1990

Soozi Holbeche, *The Power of Gems and Crystals*, Piatkus, 1989

Ni Hua-Ching, *Tao*, The Shrine of the Eternal Breath of Tao, 1988

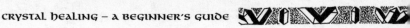
Anodes Judith, *Wheels of Life*, Llewellyn, 1995

Melody, *Love is in the Earth*, Melody, 1995

Katrina Raphaell, *Crystal Enlightenment*, Aurora Press, 1985; *Crystal Healing*, Aurora Press, 1987 and *The Crystalline Transmission*, Aurora Press, 1990

Uma Sibley, *The Complete Crystal Guide book*, Bantam, 1987

Kevin Sullivan, *Crystal Handbook*, Signet, 1987

Also

*The Illustrated Encyclopedia of Minerals and Rocks*, Promotional Reprint Co, 1977